In Search of Serenity

From Foster Child to Adoptive Mum

SALLY J KING

IN SEARCH OF SERENITY

Edited and Developed by Brenda L Andres
Cover Design by Janine Stowe Design
Cover Photo by Tyson King

Paperback ISBN: 9798690128098

eBook ISBN: 9781393363811

D-K Publishers
Canada
Printed in the United States of America
www.sallyjking.com

CONTENTS

Dedication

To Serenity. I hear you. I see you. I love you. I am you.

To Brady and Tyson for starting me off in the parenting arena with so much fun and adventure.

To Murray, who from the minute you met me, you have always been my soft place to fall.

SPECIAL ACKNOWLEDGEMENT to Brenda Andres, my editor and friend! This book would never have happened if it had not been for you. Thank you for convincing me that my story had value and needed to be told, for going above and beyond, and for allowing me to really feel heard.

SPECIAL ACKNOWLEDGEMENT to Kim Long. Until you came along as my therapist and enacted a miracle, I was embarrassed by my story. I wrote it but wasn't ready to share it. Thank you, Kim, for walking me home

INTRODUCTION

Things don't happen to you; they happen for you.
~ WHITNEY MORFITT, PHYSIOTHERAPIST

***

I WRITE THIS BOOK FOR SERENITY. I write so my voice may be heard and that one day, Serenity will know I have always heard hers. This book began because I know what it is like to be unheard. To be the problem child. Until I learned as an adult that I have Fetal Alcohol Spectrum Disorder (FASD), I had always believed that I was just a shitty person. I vowed to never let another child feel as hopeless and unlovable as I felt all my life.

A parent once said to me, "It's like you love our kids and you don't even know them." That's because I do! I love all kids. I especially don't want any child to feel the way I did. They shouldn't have to scream for help in the most unlovable ways. This book is a voice for the voiceless, the unheard, the labelled. If you insist on calling us broken, know that the only thing broken is our hearts from sheer neglect and the damage of diminishing labels. Those labels don't help us; they scar us. They dehumanize us. They say we are something to be dealt with, not loved.

Children and adults from foster care and adoption need to be heard. Our souls are crying out for understanding and acceptance. I am giving us a platform and a megaphone. I am giving us a voice. Our needs are vast and our experiences abysmal, beyond anything you could ever imagine from your safe living room. We are floundering and need your compassion. Our pain and unspeakable trauma runs deep, still we cope the best we can with the resources we have. We are not a commodity to be controlled by social services, helpless to decide what is best for us.

All children are unique, but in the child-rearing arena, a 'child from hard places' is a unicorn. It is a ridiculous notion to lump children into a predefined box and equate them developmentally, emotionally and behaviourally. The mantle does not fit, and it sets children up to fail.

An adoption coordinator once told me, "Sally, forget anything you know about raising bio kids. Throw it out. Those rules no longer apply."

What applies to a biological child does not apply to us adoptees and foster kids. We are not the same. We think differently, act differently and react differently. Even when we act out atrociously, we need patience. Even when we are unlovable, we need love. In the hardest moments, we need softness. When we are a bewildering anomaly, we need empathy. Trust me, we will search for love in the most unlovable ways. We will demand your patience at the worst times and in the worst ways.

We do not need harsh discipline and unforgiving consequences. But I promise you, if the status quo is maintained, we will continue to fall short of societal expectations. We will struggle to succeed and face daily frustrations and disappointments. We will be miserable, depressed and crushed. And we most certainly will not thrive. All of the misguided discipline, battles, fights and consequences will be for naught, because our behaviour is not the full picture. There is so much more you need to know.

I am also writing for those who think they know what is best for the foster and adopted child. If you are thinking of embarking on a journey to foster or adopt, do not do it lightly. We are children with traumatic beginnings, dealing with wounds and despicable circumstances beyond our comprehension. We do not care that someone *thinks* they know what is best for us, we only care desperately that someone loves us through our circumstances.

We are a peculiar breed, but we are also fabulous, and we deserve better than just a second chance. By sharing my personal experiences as one of those fostered and adopted children, I strive to turn my mess into a message. Maybe I cannot right the wrongs of my childhood, but

I can address the glaring flaws of a broken system in the hope of bringing change. I also pray that the knowledge I have gained from the trenches of the foster system can be a beacon in the darkness for someone who is reading this for answers and hope.

So, open yourself to new possibilities and accept that you are (most likely) in over your head. My approach and techniques may be foreign and may go against everything you've ever believed about fostering and adoption, but then again, if nothing else seems to be working, it might be worth a try.

CHAPTER 1

Growing up Adopted

Life is pain, highness. Anyone who says differently is selling something.
~ WILLIAM GOLDMAN, The Princess Bride

SERENITY... I HAVE BEEN SEARCHING for it my entire life—that elusive sense of peace and self-acceptance. Who knew it would come to me, wrapped up in a tiny girl with big brown eyes, who had no one?

I am a foster child and an adoptee. Much speculation surrounds my birth, but I know for certain that I was breech when I tumbled into this world on September 17, 1964 and was given the name Cheryl Lynn Friesen. I only lived with my birth mother for the first five months of my life until she was reported to be neglecting and starving me. For my own protection, I was seized into custody by Canadian Child Welfare Services and situated into foster care. Once they had 'fattened me up' to a healthy weight, I was placed for adoption. At six months of age, Jean and Allan Dick adopted and renamed me, Sally-Jean Dick.

Throughout my young life, something felt missing, like a puzzle piece lost from the box. There were no early baby pictures of me. It was always a subtle reminder of the unmentionable years. I thought of it as B.A. and A.A. *Before-Adoption* and *After-Adoption*. I spent the better part of fifty years trying to find that missing piece. I spent a lifetime trying to fill the hole it created during those first six months of my story and fighting the terrible circumstances of my entry into the world.

A TABOO SUBJECT

On a logical level, I was aware that I had a good home and knew that my parents loved me, but there remained a strange void I could not shake. I think that adoption becomes a taboo subject, like the elephant in the room. Everyone sees it. Everyone knows it is there, but no one mentions it, as if holding a collective breath, drawing attention even more.

At an early age, the shadow of my adoption was evident to me. It may have appeared to others as the picture-perfect childhood, but darkness lurked beneath my fragile surface. I had been *taken from my mother*. That childhood wound cut deeper than anyone knew. No matter what else happened growing up, that terrible knowledge always lingered. A little voice in my head whispered, *You are not wanted. You are not enough. You are not one of them.*

Comments concerning my origins and opinions about adoption swirled around me. Maybe no one ever intended to be cruel, but the words cut like razors. I overheard them and I understood. I was not the first choice. I was the lesser option of infertility. I was second best.

No one wants to be second best. Everyone wants the blue ribbon. To be the personification of a consolation prize is a bitter pill to swallow.

THE STARK TRUTH IN THE MIRROR

All anyone wants is a sense of belonging, but for someone who is adopted, that feeling is fleeting. No matter how many declarations or promises or assurances we are given, we doubt. We feel out of place. I experienced life on the periphery looking in, feeling like I was not truly part of the happy family unit.

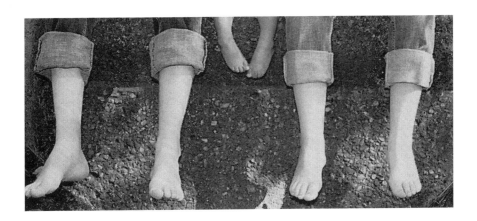

The stark truth stared at me in the mirror. I did not look like the rest of my family. My adoptive family was dark-haired, olive-skinned and brown-eyed. I was blonde, blue-eyed, and big for my age. It was like wearing a sign that screamed: *This child is not a part of us.*

Even my adopted brother Graeme appeared more like our Mum and Dad in colouring and physique. Graeme, I always thought, blended into the family picture while I stuck out as proof. While their physical characteristics unified them, mine did not. As an adopted child, this mattered to me so desperately.

No amount of reassurance could convince me otherwise. I knew that I was different; I felt like I didn't belong.

I was adopted second into the household. A four-year gap separated my brother and me. Too far apart in age to grow up as friends, the disparity was close enough that jealousy and animosity festered. Graeme had been the centre of our parents' universe for five years until I came along and stole his spotlight. A relentless battle overshadowed our childhood years. I honestly felt inferior to my brother and he regularly displayed his contempt by terrorizing me. Most would call it sibling rivalry, but for me it was horrid. Sadly, it is a conflict we still wage as adults. So much has transpired between us and, as some would say, too much water under the bridge. In truth, it is much more than either of us has any desire to repair.

SCHOOL BULLIES AND TRAUMA KIDS

School proved to be its own brutal reality. Each day would start with a stressful early morning rush to get out the door, and then for the next several hours I was confined to the relentless overstimulation of crowded classrooms. It is not an exaggeration to say that I hated school. My circa 1970s teachers had no clue how to recognize a trauma kid or how to educate a child with learning challenges. I had no social game, either. My classmates taunted and terrified me, even though I tried outrageously to relate to them.

I remember actually trying to get sick so I could stay home. Nothing was better than the silver-lined cloud of catching a cough and cold each winter. I reveled in that reprieve and would drag it out for as long as possible. I could make a stay at home stretch for two weeks.

Looking back, I now recognize that I had Attention Deficit Disorder (ADD), though none of us knew it at the time. I daily found myself in trouble because I couldn't sit still or be quiet. In the lower grades my teacher would banish me to the corner, and on really bad days, tape my mouth shut (yes, that really happened several times).

I vividly recall sitting in the corner of the classroom, tape pinched across my dry lips, and struggling to breathe through a plugged nose from allergies. I had dared to peel up a corner of the tape from my lips to gasp for air, when my teacher turned and caught me in the act.

Without allowing me a chance to explain, she scolded my "disobedience" in front of all my classmates and added more time to my punishment. Mocking laughter swirled around me and hot tears stung my eyes. I grew to dread the humiliation of school.

Every day my anxiety shot through the roof. I struggled to avoid low marks, but I always had such a hard time with the schoolwork. I often cried from the shear stress and frustration of having to perform. Whenever I think back to my school days, I feel a deep hatred. Even now, as I recall the memory of tape across my lips, a knot clenches my stomach. Maybe what upsets me most is that schools haven't really come that far today. Kids from hard places are still misunderstood and are still considered a problem.

My childhood outside of the home was tumultuous, to say the least. While struggling to fit in with my peers, I was often bullied for being different. I began to comfort-eat all the time and soon my weight became another issue.

Friendships were a constant source of conflict. I spent so much of my life being scared of what I perceived would be an eventual rejection that I usually ended up with so-called friends that blatantly used me. Admittedly, I did not handle it very well either.

I came to believe that I was undeserving of true friends. Consequently, most of the time I was terrified of social rejection. I thought I had to earn people's love and acceptance to deserve any semblance of personal validation. I tried to be the funniest, the most helpful, the most supportive. It was all, quite frankly, exhausting.

Let me tell you, drowning in a friendship is a uniquely dreadful situation. I would take it upon myself to maintain so much of the relationship that eventually I became drained and angry. My pattern was to give and give and give until ultimately, I grew to resent the very expectations I had created. Relationships frequently ended in a disastrous explosion because I would completely self-combust.

JUST AN UNDIAGNOSED BRAT

When I was a foster child, no one really understood about childhood trauma. No one talked about attachment issues, prenatal exposure to drugs and alcohol, sensory processing disorders, or even ADD. My parents were just flying completely by the seat of their pants. They had no clue of what they were in for and were thoroughly unequipped for the maelstrom they had taken on. I know they tried to raise us kids the best they could, but the harsh discipline advice from family and friends only added to the frustrations I am sure they experienced while raising my brother and me.

I was the spoiled, contentious brat. I was the kid no one wanted around. In reality, I was simply a stressed, misunderstood and misjudged little girl who didn't know how to handle the world around me. I was a child with unresolved issues that, in those days, no one knew about or understood. I loathed crowds; I hated loud noises. I couldn't cope with the chaotic explosion of emotions that burst inside me when stimulus flew at me all at once. I literally derailed on a regular basis. It wasn't like I wanted to flip out and throw a tantrum, but in the moment, there was no control or conscious thought. It was only a furious, blind instinct. I could not stop myself.

After my explosion was over, I would drown in regret and self-hatred. It was a hideous path that I would walk again and again throughout my life. In so many of the situations that I look back upon, I recognize how turbulent my childhood truly was.

You may be too young to remember a TV show called *Family Affair*, but it was a popular sitcom when I was a kid. It starred a little girl named Buffy with curly blonde ponytails. When Mum brushed my own curly blonde hair into ponytails, naturally everyone would call me Buffy. This didn't bother me, but the teasing sometimes went too far.

My family used to go camping all the time with the same group of people and there was one guy who persistently goaded me just to get a reaction. He would come up to me and tug my ponytails. Every single time he did it, I would lose my junk! Had my parents known this action was triggering for a child with sensory processing disorder who couldn't emotionally filter it, they would have recognized my 'bad behaviour' for what it was. Instead of asking him to stop, I was punished for being a holy terror and sent to the trailer.

During my childhood and teen years, whenever I was thrust into a high pressure or unfair situation, I inevitably responded poorly. I recognize now that it was simply way too much for me to process. I have spent far too much time beating myself up for what I had no control over. All through my childhood and even all into my adult years I felt misunderstood. I knew no one understood me, but worse, I sensed they didn't want to. If they had, would it have made enough difference to alter the course of events that occurred next?

THE SECRET NO ONE WOULD BELIEVE

When I was ten years old my dad's sister, with whom our whole family was extremely close, married a British man who had moved from England to be a driver for my dad's trucking company. My aunt was smitten, and all the family thought he was wonderful, but I did not get along with him at all. Everyone assumed my aversion was because I was an insufferable brat.

The reality was darker and far more insidious than anyone's imagination. This 'favourite' uncle had begun to sexually molest me. Every chance he could, he stole my innocence, and I couldn't tell anyone. No one would listen; who would believe me? How could I reveal something so shocking and disgraceful that he had convinced me was my fault anyway? Instead, I was rude and insolent to my uncle in public. But in private, he threatened me to silence; his abuse was monstrous and relentless.

There was no getting away from him. I was terrified and felt unsafe all the time. He was *everywhere*. Nearly every day he came to our house—both he and my aunt worked for my dad—and most weekends they visited with my parents to share meals and drink heavily. For five years, I lived in fear of every family gathering. Every Christmas, every Easter, every birthday, every *freaking* weekend, my uncle would be there!

Even worse, when my parents went away, they left me with my aunt and uncle. With no spare bedroom, I had to sleep in the open on their living room floor. In the night, he would covertly slip in and lay on the floor beside me; somehow my aunt always slept through it. There was no safe place. Even in broad daylight, he found a way. There was no escape.

Then, suddenly in the summer of grade eight, as I was turning thirteen, I grew three inches. All at once I had grown tall enough to fend off my uncle's attacks. It was a heady relief, but I still was not safe. Undeterred by this new ability to oppose him, he still managed to corner me at unexpected moments brushing against me with filthy gestures and disgusting innuendos. My skin crawls to this day when I think of his hot breath and raspy whispers.

Perhaps the connection was ingrained early on that if I was big enough, I could be protected. *If I could put an armour of fat around me*, I thought, *maybe it would protect me.* This was the desire of my subconscious mind, but the voice of my conscious mind taunted, *you are so fat, you are disgusting, you are worthless.* I believe that was the beginning of my lifelong battle with food and my weight that, even now in my fifties, I still wage.

All of the adults in my family seemed to drink heavily. In fact, alcohol played such a major part of my childhood that I can recall being five years old and my dad letting me sip his beer. Maybe they thought it was funny, but I learned to get a taste for alcohol early. It became my method of coping with the confusion, anger, fear and abuse to binge eat and secretly drink.

MY RAPIDLY IMPLODING WORLD

Events took an even darker turn in my life when I was eighteen years old. My mother, the one person whom I always believed truly had my back, died unexpectedly right after Christmas.

From the moment she sat me down at age fifteen to tell me she had breast cancer, she became a different person, focused only on surviving the disease. From that moment on, nothing would ever be the same again. Mum was almost in denial. After undergoing a radical double mastectomy, chemo and radiation, she was convinced she was going to beat this, and we all believed her. For two and a half years she fought hard against all the odds, telling everyone, "I'm fine. I'm not going anywhere."

In the final three months before she died, I don't think she was right in her mind. She began to behave wretchedly toward me. It is miserable to recall, but I now believe that she feared I was immature and not ready to go it alone. And frankly, she was right. I depended too much upon her. Maybe she turned ugly on me as her way of toughening me up quickly.

It was a horrifying time and my world was rapidly imploding. Everyone around me seemed to think they knew best and took the liberty of informing me of what I was doing wrong.

The worst part was that I had absolutely nowhere to turn. I had no one. Exactly one month before Mum died, my boyfriend whom I truly loved and believed I would marry, dumped me for someone else. It was beyond impossible to try and process this while I was losing my mother.

After Mum passed, I lost my dad too. He seemed to go crazy, drinking heavily and forbidding us to talk about her. If it was even possible, Dad became a worse alcoholic than before. Then, a mere two weeks after Mum's funeral, Dad abruptly took off to Reno, Nevada with another woman. I was beyond shocked and devastated, never mind the slap in the face to Mum's memory. Was that all she had meant to him after thirty years?

When I look back now with a clearer head, I understand that Dad was completely desolate. The unthinkable had happened and he'd lost his life partner. Maybe he felt that he needed to replace her with someone as quickly as possible. After her death, there were moments when I would walk into the living room and he would be sitting silently, drinking and playing solitaire.

There was something achingly symbolic about him playing solitaire that just ripped my heart out. I knew he was in so much pain, but Dad was from a generation where you didn't talk about feelings; you just got on with life. He had nowhere to place his anguish and devastation other than the relief of a bottle and in a card game for one.

To this day I still see the scene perfectly in my head. His workworn hands lay out the cards and then he reaches over to grasp his glass. Rum and a deck of cards were the only solace for a suddenly widowed fifty-two-year-old man with no other way to process an unbearable loss.

Funny, I always picture my dad so old in that moment, yet he was the same age that I am now. It took me many years to be able to see him as just a broken man who was lost in grief and utter desolation. Dad was a human being and not the superman I had built him up to be. At the time, he handled everything terribly, and we battled—hard. There were nightly fights and endless bickering. Dad did not approve of my choices and I did not approve of his. We were at a stalemate; two people overwhelmed with sorrow and bitterness and nowhere to place it other than to vent anger on each other.

And vent we did! We argued hotly; we agreed on nothing. Gone was the endearing man that exuded excitement like a kid on Christmas morning. Gone was the man who taught his little girl to dance. Gone were all my sweet childhood memories of a loving daddy. Gone. Fallen down a bottle. Replaced by anger, resentment and depravity. Replaced by hate and venom and oh so much drinking, for both of us. My mother, my rock, was gone. And now my daddy, my superhero, was gone as well. My childhood was ripped away, only to be replaced by this! Agony swathed in anguish and wrapped up in a fireball of drunken rage.

DROWNING IN ANXIETY AND ANGUISH

I hate myself to this day and regret the way I felt towards my Mum while she was dying. I could not handle the pressure and stress of the situation and I know I responded badly to some of the events that occurred. Mum was my everything; she was leaving me, and I was furious. I felt like I was drowning in anxiety and anguish. The water was closing in on my life and I could not bear it or save myself. And then she died. And then my Dad went crazy and wouldn't talk about her. He wanted to pretend she didn't exist. But how? How can you pretend that the most important person in your world did not exist?

I rebelled. We fought and we battled, and we screamed. We fractured our relationship beyond repair. When my dad and I weren't fighting, I would lay in bed and beat myself up for everything I had said. I was this drowning girl and nobody, and I mean not one fucking person, would throw me a life preserver. Instead, they just told me I was wrong. Once again, I was alone in the world, and I had never felt lonelier in my entire life. Those were some of my darkest days. I fell back on the only coping mechanism I had ever learned from my parents. I drank to forget. I slept around to try to feel something— *anything*. But the truth was, I was numb. Nothing could make me feel better, or anything at all, for that matter. I felt dead inside. I thought maybe that would be the solution.

For several years after Mum died, I floundered. Literally drifting through life, I moved from one thing to another. Nothing stuck. Different universities, different friends, different men. Nothing filled the empty hole that had been shot through me like a gaping wound. I was depressed and hopeless. Twice in my life, I had lost a mother figure. Twice, that bond was shattered. I now know it is a wound that never, ever heals. My life would never be the same. Once again, I became a problem. No one knew what to do with me. My soul was crushed, and my heart was broken beyond repair. I was flailing in the wind, out of control.

CHAPTER 2

In Search of Prince Charming

I just figured if I'm going to be a mess, might as well be a hot mess, right?
~ MINDY KALING, The Mindy Project

I BECAME A SHELL OF MY FORMER SELF. I grieved hard for my mother; the toughest part was going through it alone. During this time, I began suffering from debilitating migraines, but in my depleted state, it seemed just another card in the rotten hand I was dealt.

I drifted through my life in a solitary state, mastering the art of being alone and lonely in a room full of people. I remained safely guarded, never revealing how I really felt or what mattered to me. I would agree with everything people said and adapt my thoughts and opinions to suit others. So, you can imagine how successful I was at dating. I allowed men to treat me like utter garbage. They used me, abused me, and messed with my heart before moving on. This became my normal. It was all I knew, and I think subconsciously I sought out emotionally unavailable men. I certainly didn't have to look far; they were everywhere. The reality is, I never believed I would ever meet my Prince Charming.

OUT OF CONTROL

I felt trapped in the "fight, flight or freeze" prison in my mind, established all those years ago as a baby who had no choice or say in what would happen to her. I clearly remember, after Mum died, cleaning the house so meticulously that you could have eaten off the floors. In retrospect, so much of my world was out of control that cleaning was the one thing I could manage, so manage it I did. I thought that by keeping her house immaculate I was validating Mum and somehow keeping her alive. It was a new way of coping and I needed it to dull my pain somehow. In every other way, I felt so out of control, that ultimately, I surrendered to others in my life to make decisions for me.

I became a compulsive people pleaser, so much so that I let people stomp all over me and take advantage. One night at the University of Lethbridge, a couple of guys who I had considered my friends attempted to rape me in the hall after a late-night party. They grabbed me from either side—trapping me—and began to tear off my clothes. I was terrified and screamed as I struggled. Another male friend came down the hall just in time. He shoved them away and escorted me safely out of there.

You want to know what low self-esteem is? It is lending your car the next day to the same two guys who attempted to rape you. That, folks, is a special brand of fucked up. I mean *seriously?* I knew deep down their actions were reprehensible, even criminal, yet I wanted them to like me and not be mad at me. Read that again: *I was worried these two lowlifes would be mad at me!* That is how distorted my thinking had become. I despised myself and hated my life. I just wanted my Mum. I wanted that soft place to fall, but it was out of reach for me. There was no soft place to fall because I was unlovable, and I was undeserving.

After that incident, I spiraled down even farther. I was a hot mess. I failed out of three different universities, spent too much money, drank and partied too much, and used food as my escape, all to mask the incredible pain that was my existence. Sure, there were fleeting moments that made me happy but deep happiness eluded me. I spent my entire life apologizing for my existence. I would leave conversations feeling empty and horrible because I had said the wrong thing or was too forceful, too passionate, too mouthy. The problem always laid in my need to feel validated and understood. That small child trapped inside me screamed to be heard. I'd think, *If I just say this one more thing, they will get me.* I wanted to feel at home in my own skin, but I never felt confident in who I was. I only felt hollow and empty.

STRIKE THREE BUT NOT OUT

It was while I was struggling in my third disastrous attempt at university as a hopeless bid to honour my Mum's wishes, that I finally discovered a passion that I could make into a career. I had created a side gig of cutting hair for drinking cash and I realized that this was something I was good at and actually enjoyed. So, I enrolled at the LA School of Hair Design in Lethbridge and began working as a stylist. My personal life was in tatters, but in my career, I could seek success and validation.

When the opportunity came to become a national haircutting artist for Paul Mitchell, the comedic mask that I wore so well was just what they wanted. As my popularity grew, I felt lonelier. There is nothing like feeling alone on a stage in Montreal in front of ten thousand people. Though my work brought a measure of satisfaction and worth, my personal relationships continued to be fractured and screwed up. The murky years that followed were a litany of trying to look for love in all the wrong places in a misguided quest for love, acceptance and belonging.

I reached an all-time low when one night my boyfriend's father showed up drunk at my house. Like a gruesome flashback, he threw himself on me and suddenly I was wrestling off another attempted rape.

Through sheer force of will, I fought back and forced him out, but not before he had trashed furniture, kicked holes in the wall, and nearly tore the door off its hinges. When I called my boyfriend, crying that his father had tried to rape me, I expected him to be furious and rush over to rescue me, but instead, the disbelief was acid in his voice.

"There is no way that happened, and if it did, you must have provoked him!" Then he dropped the final bomb, "And anyway, why are you telling me? It's not my problem."

Once again, it was evident I was on my own. I barely slept that night. My door wouldn't close, so I braced it with a bungee cord. I lay huddled and terrified on the couch by my broken door, clutching a baseball bat.

The next morning, feeling desperate but also angry, I knew that I was finished with my boyfriend. My nonexistent self-worth had allowed yet another man to use and abuse me, disregarding my needs for his own selfish agenda. If I persisted on this path of self-destruction, I knew I would not see thirty-five. I had what you might call a "come to Jesus meeting." I finally made a decision that would change my life. From that moment I was done with the kind of men I had always thought of as "my type." Never again would I subject myself to unfulfilling garbage relationships!

WHAT DOES HE WANT WITH ME?

Why is it that when you stop looking, you find what you desired all along? By the time I turned thirty I had long since given up on relationships with men. Then, just when I let it all go, along came Prince Charming. The day I met Murray King,

I was actually shocked by how generous and considerate he was. This man was confident and content within his own skin, but not in an arrogant or cocky way. He was just completely comfortable within himself and did not seem concerned by what anyone else thought of him. This concept was so foreign to me that I couldn't begin to comprehend it. Murray was a complete enigma to me.

One of my hairstyling clients became insistent about hooking me up with her mechanic who was single and would be "perfect for me." I wasn't interested in dating anyone, let alone her greasy, knuckle-dragging mechanic friend. Apparently, he wasn't all that enthusiastic about dating her "bimbo hairstylist," either. But after dodging my client's relentless coaxing, Murray and I both reluctantly agreed to meet each other. Since at the time we worked opposite shifts, we could only talk on the telephone at first. It was three weeks before we finally met in person.

At first, I couldn't understand what Murray could possibly see in me. Why would such a remarkable man want *me*? The legacy of my birth mother's neglect and rejection, multiplied by the years of abuse and pain, had thrashed my pathetic self-esteem to rubble. Then along came this amazing man who didn't care about my past, and even more astonishingly, did not treat me as damaged goods.

From the beginning, Murray seemed too good to be true. Somehow this man loved and desired me for me, warts and all. He treated me with such treasured respect that I could actually believe this was a man who had no agenda. Murray saw me for who I was, and it turns out he loved it! I had never experienced that before. It took a while before I could fully breathe and not secretly worry that he would one day leave me.

Enveloped in his unconditional love, my defenses tumbled down. For the first time in my life, here was a tall, strong man who made me feel safe, and yet he was also kind and sensitive. He was one of the gentlest human beings I had ever met. Murray became my soft place to fall. Like a cheesy song, he *completed* me, and I didn't feel like I had to do this life alone anymore. I had a life partner, a best friend. Murray truly got me even more than I knew myself. For the first time since my mum died, not only did I feel safe, I felt loved.

After nearly twenty-five years of marriage, I still thank my lucky stars every day that God put Murray in my life. Right from the start, I always felt as if Mum chose him for me. When I learned that his birthday was also the same day as hers, I knew. He was the one! Life did not suddenly become easy for me, though. There are no fairy tales. There were still issues to resolve, and marriage brought its own set of complications, but one thing I knew for sure was that with Murray by my side I could do anything.

CHAPTER 3

A Family of Kings

Sometimes you just have to throw on a crown
and remind them who you're dealing with.
~ (attributed to) MARILYN MONROE

WHEN MURRAY AND I WERE FIRST MARRIED we lived in Okotoks, a small town south of Calgary. I became pregnant on our honeymoon and it seemed like we had the world by the tail. Together we built a new house, bonding over home projects. Then abruptly, three months into my pregnancy, I began to bleed. An ultrasound confirmed that our precious and beautiful baby was dead. I was devastated. I couldn't process it. My joy evaporated into horror and dark thoughts clawed back into my mind.

"Don't get attached, Sally. Don't expect anything. Nothing good ever happens to you. Don't let the universe know you are happy, Sally because as soon as you feel safe, the world immediately crashes in."

PAYBACK IS A BITCH

I grew obsessed with becoming pregnant again. Each month the news was the same. Not this time. All of our friends were getting pregnant before me. I wanted to be happy for them, but my pain was so raw. Everywhere I went, all I saw were expectant mothers.

One bleak day after seeing what seemed like a dozen pregnant women in Costco, I sat in the car and sobbed to Murray, "Is every woman in Calgary pregnant but me?"

Loss and longing blurred the next year of trying until, all at once, I was nauseous and began to vomit. In spite of feeling dreadfully ill, I was ecstatic. I gratefully settled in for nine months of puking and growing a human. In March of 1998, Brady came into the world via scheduled C-section, footling breech. When they cut into me, they cut his heel. It struck me powerfully as I held him that this tiny human was our own child—a genetic link to us—and my soul felt complete.

Murray and I finally had our little family. Brady was an easy baby who grew to be a sweet-natured toddler, always happy and giggling. When I became pregnant with our second child two-and-a-half years later, I was absolutely convinced that "she" would be a girl. It was a genuine surprise when our son joined us with outdoor plumbing! Far from disappointment, we were simply astonished. Tyson was born in the middle of a massive blizzard in November 2000, and it should have been forewarning for this tornado child that we were about to raise. He thrust into the world as if announcing, "I'm here! The party has arrived! Buckle up!"

Tyson was a force to be reckoned with. Busy and strong-willed, he was just like his Mum. He pushed boundaries like nothing I had ever seen. As an infant, he only wanted me and would pass up Murray for Mum every time. Brady was an uncomplicated, laid-back little human who rarely needed disciplining, but as Tyson moved to the terrible twos, we found that punitive discipline made every situation much worse. Instead, we learned to be creative in our approach to raising two very different little boys.

Once at a family gathering, one of my cousins met our two-year-old whirlwind for the first time. While watching Tyson command the show, my cousin grinned cheekily and said, "Wow payback is a bitch hey, Sal?"

IGNORANCE IS NOT BLISS

I had blundered into motherhood thinking, *no problem, I got this!* I was a busy mom with a fast food habit and a heavy reliance on pre-packaged food that was devoid of nutrition. Our uncomplicated first baby left us unprepared when our second son's needs stopped us in our tracks. Tyson was born allergic to life. He did not sleep well, and he had eczema so bad he would scratch his skin raw until it looked like hamburger. At eighteen months of age, we discovered Tyson had anaphylaxis to peanuts. When acute asthma followed soon after, my world was rocked!

Knowing something had to change, I began to read the unpronounceable ingredient labels on the food I was preparing. An awareness dawned. How could I continue to feed my boys all these chemicals and think it was ok? This launched an in-depth research tangent, only to discover the utter dysfunction of our North American food system. I threw out the pre-packaged crap and started creating my own healthy recipes. I knew I was onto something when friends, and even teachers, started phoning me to talk about what my kids were having in their lunchboxes.

Lunches, I discovered, were the bane of every mother's existence. Mums were looking for concrete ideas that were simple to prepare without a lot of hard-to-find ingredients. The idea of writing a cookbook formed, and within a few months of compiling and testing recipes, *LunchBox Love* was born. Best of all, as I began to cook fresh whole food, Tyson's debilitating eczema began to disappear. Even though inhalers and EpiPens were still part of his life, we no longer had to live in constant fear of what he was eating.

PONYTAILS AND TEA PARTIES

Our lives settled into a busy routine. My cookbook began to sell, and as I received reader responses, I decided to start a blog to respond to frequently asked questions. It was a natural progression to begin holding cooking classes at local health food stores. I should have been content. My wonderful little family was healthier, and I was making a difference by helping other Mums.

But a growing disquiet burned in my soul. Perhaps it was because my mother-daughter relationship had been cut short by Mum's death. Whatever the reason, I harboured a deep desire for a little girl to bridge that gap. I yearned for pretty dresses, ponytails, dolls and tea parties. I could not explain it, and no amount of logic or reason would quiet the severe longing. I *ached* for a daughter. But as more and more time passed, it became apparent that we were not getting pregnant again.

FINDING THE PUZZLE PIECE

The longing persisted and I began to entertain a new idea. I thought I would have a difficult job convincing my husband, but by the time I started throwing around the idea of adoption, Murray had already come to the same conclusion. *Was this how I would find the missing piece in the puzzle of my life?*

Murray and I never imagined that we would adopt. It was not our plan, but I sensed God was gently pushing us to adoption. It wasn't quick and easy, though. The process was grueling and at times incredibly painful. None of the different paths to adoption come without pitfalls and our journey was fraught with heartache and frustration. We came achingly close to completing a private adoption when apparently, we were considered too old. Of course, they only told us this after taking a bunch of our money.

After private adoption failed to pan out, we learned about international adoption and its rapid process. The costs involved were enormous, but what price tag do you place on a daughter? We knew of China's strict population control laws that limit families to one child, so adopting a baby girl from China was a natural and heart-tugging choice. However, the complications surrounding international adoption proved to be insurmountable.

The timing of our application to the China Center of Adoption Affairs was unfortunate. In 2007, China enacted stricter criteria for adoption, and then with the approach of the 2008 Beijing Olympics, suddenly all adoptions were halted. Perhaps under the microscope of world opinion, they were scrambling to deflect the poor image created by their huge annual adoption numbers, 90% of them unwanted girls. We were back to the drawing board.

We had exhausted all avenues, it seemed. As the years passed, I despaired that my dream of a little girl would never be realized. On our fifteenth anniversary, Murray took me away for the weekend to celebrate, but it seemed like we spent most of our time expressing disappointment and bitterness over our lack of adoption results. I was feeling strongly that we couldn't let our desire for a daughter fade. Sharing his own frustration, Murray agreed.

It was a heartbreaking weekend that just left us feeling helpless to know what step to take next. Defeated, we returned home that Sunday night, and the next morning Murray flew to North Dakota for work.

DON'T HOLD YOUR BREATH

Life continued, as it must with two small boys, and I settled into the routine of daily tasks. I had begun homeschooling our boys, so along with blogging and cooking classes, I kept myself busy. It was then, when it seemed all hope was lost, when not having a daughter was becoming our reality, that a phone call changed all our lives.

Serenity came into our world on a warm August morning in 2011. I had been out running errands when my cell phone rang. It was a friend calling to tell me of a little girl that a friend of a friend of a friend, was fostering. They were seeking a permanent home for her and it appeared as though she was going to be eligible for adoption.

You have to understand, I have had those calls before and they never amounted to anything except discouragement, so I did not hold out hope. I carried on with my day, but as I headed home with a phone number in my hand, I already knew that I would call.

After ending the conversation with the child's foster nana, I was uniquely enthused. This time felt different, somehow. Murray's flight in from work was due at 1:36 p.m. that afternoon.

I called him at 1:40 p.m. I could wait no longer. He was still waiting to exit the airplane when I reached him, so I quickly explained the situation. We agreed that I should make the arrangements to meet with the foster family and the tiny nine-month-old girl that same night.

TAKING THE LONG SHOT

It was a long shot, but I was excited and incredibly nervous. Murray arrived home and we restlessly attempted to keep ourselves busy for several hours. Finally, we loaded the boys into the van and drove to Edmonton. Joe and Suzanne, the baby's foster parents, were incredibly gracious when we arrived and crowded into their living room. There, in the midst of our circle, sat a tiny brown-eyed doll with two black ponytails sticking up. I could not tear my eyes off her.

Serenity's chicklet teeth grinned a bright-white smile against her dark skin and her whole face lit up. Gazing back at her, my heart lurched. I was smitten. *This is my child.* I instantly moved to pick her up. Tyson and Brady, who were ten and twelve at the time, interacted with her almost immediately and all at once we were fighting over who would hold her. There are only two other moments that compare with the surreal experience of meeting Serenity for the first time. Those were when my boys were born and placed on my breast. Although the circumstances of their delivery were different, this passion that consumed me was the same—instant, unconditional love! This was the daughter I had longed for all those years.

Leaving Joe and Suzanne's house that night without that little girl in my arms nearly destroyed me. As we walked out of the door and paused on their front steps, Murray turned to look at me and said, "Sally, she is ours!"

I thought my heart would burst and jump out of my chest. He'd had the same reaction. *He knew it too.* We simply had to find a way to bring her home.

At the time, I did not foresee the battle we would wage in order to make this little girl part of our family. We started visiting her every other night. It was both beautiful and bittersweet. Leaving without her at the end of each visit was excruciating. It pained me to be away from Serenity, even for a day. I craved her. I never wanted her to think we would not be there for her. I now understand that none of our adoption efforts had panned-out prior to that night because our sweet girl was not ready for us; she hadn't been born yet. I can still hear my mum, with her gorgeous English accent, *Patience is a virtue Sally-Jean.* We would require herculean patience in our wait for her. But wait we would.

DESTINED TO BE A KING

When we found Serenity, we were so in love that we knew we had to break life and limb to bring her home. I knew deep in my soul that this was my child—*my daughter.* I knew it like I knew I was still breathing. So, I was shocked and incredibly hurt by the reactions of some of our friends and family to our plan to adopt. Many of them just did not understand or have compassion in their hearts to comprehend our choice. This was not a house or a car ... Serenity was a child, a tiny girl who had already lost so much in her short life.

Ok, it wasn't what they would have chosen for themselves. I get that, but this was what Murray and I had decided for our family, and we are grown-ass adults, dammit. Why did it seem that everyone was set against it and felt the need to crap on our decision with their negative and unsolicited opinions? Mostly I was devastated by the apparent belief that this child was disposable, that she wasn't a real person, that she wasn't deserving of a forever family. We weren't asking for their opinion, but I was determined to prove them wrong.

I would like to be able to say that our adoption experience was a walk in the park with no issues and no complications. Alas, not so. While in so many ways it was beautiful and exciting, it was also an incredibly gut-wrenching and callous pilgrimage. What proved most challenging throughout were the countless frustrating situations created by a rigid and archaic foster system and its high-handed staff. But I will always maintain that it has been worth every stressful minute.

Through no fault of her own, Serenity was ensnared by the circumstances of her birth, but our little girl would not be defined by her past. In every way, we were now her family and we would be her protectors. The unconditional love my husband and I felt for this child the moment we met her was no different than what we knew as biological parents and the love we felt for our boys through pregnancy and birth. We simply knew that we must have her. She was destined to be a King. She was destined to be our sweet princess. Funny enough, I believe God was sending me that message in her name. She was something I had always been searching for... Serenity. We were, and always will be, her soft place to fall.

CHAPTER 4

Adoption Odyssey

They say what doesn't kill you makes you stronger.
At this point, I should be able to bench press a minivan.

~ UNKNOWN

THE FIRST, AND MOST IMPORTANT PART of the adoption narrative, is to recognize that it *always* derives from loss—*profound and agonizing loss.* Children who come to a family through adoption are not a blank slate. They do not start at zero. They invariably arrive with a whole cargo load of baggage. Adoptive parents, who are so excited and grateful to finally have their prayers answered in this baby, would be wise to never forget that their joy was paid for by the pain of two other people. In that pain is the loss of the first mother. It is not all rainbows and unicorns. Parents who adopt have a different situation than those who give birth, and a successful relationship with that child recognizes the difference.

BATTLING A BROKEN SYSTEM

Little did we know we had embarked upon a messy three-year odyssey of adopting through the foster system. Our joy would be marred by tears, trials, skirmishes, and power-wielding social workers with arbitrary rules and soulless policies that would damn near break me. Their system is so broken and flawed that some days I thought I could not go on. The constant stress, worry, and battle with child services and their complete disregard for Serenity's best interest exhausted me to the point of illness.

Serenity had survived the gestation and labor of a woman with a serious addiction, only to become trapped in the middle of dreadful government bureaucracy that was more concerned with arbitrary rules than her welfare.

As an added complication, Serenity came to us with Methicillin-resistant staphylococcus aureus (MRSA), an antibiotic-resistant superbug that causes difficult to treat infections in the body. Even if active infections go away after treatment, MRSA can come back repeatedly (Gonzales, n.d.) because a person colonized with MRSA can still have bacteria on their skin and in their nose. Serenity's MRSA infection manifested in swollen red boils all over her little body that became painful lesions seeping pus.

Our little girl needed someone to love her, cherish her and advocate for her, but I personally believed that few truly had this child's best interests in mind. Serenity was worth our effort; she was worth our diligence. I knew deep in my heart that God wanted me to keep fighting and to push the support workers into doing the right things. It was incredibly hard for me to accept at the time because it was evident from the outset that the well-being of a child is secondary. The support workers were militant and heavy-handed, and we seemed to disagree on everything from her medical treatment to the food we fed her. I figuratively had to push and literally had to fight to get them to do what was best for Serenity.

My desire to change this little girl's life for the better and for Serenity to beat the statistics was potent. I was hellbent on proving everyone wrong. Serenity would have an amazing life despite her grim start. She would have a life of love and purpose and happiness. She would never have to repeat the hellish cycle of her biological parents. It was my mantra from day one.

DON'T PISS OFF YOUR SOCIAL WORKER

In spite of a daunting beginning, we started on this path to adopt Serenity with the best of intentions. Everybody said to me, "Whatever you do, don't piss off your social worker." So, I approached this adventure with fear and intimidation. I felt beholden to these civil servants who seemed to hold all the power, but I was determined to do this right. My outlook was positive. I resolved to kill them with kindness and win them over with fresh baking and yummy coffee. Ah yes, such good intentions. And then I met our first support worker.

'Carol' (that is not her real name) never returned calls. She took so many days out of the office that it took seemingly forever to meet with her. When we finally had our first visit, I was terrified. Cold and business-like, the woman walked through our house with the proverbial white glove and denounced everything we were doing for Serenity.

"We are looking for *family*," she said sternly, all the while not once looking at Serenity or even attempting to engage with her. Carol was rude, pushy and invasive. It was evident that the job she had to do was more important than this child. Here was Serenity's supposed support worker? What a joke. The woman was horrid, and she left me feeling defeated and helpless.

Her second home visit was the last straw. Carol barged in demanding explanations, barking disapproval, and ran roughshod over our home and family. She provoked an argument over not having a gate on the stairs. I tried to explain that not every home has a gate, so our goal was to empower Serenity on how to climb up and down the stairs safely by herself. Carol was having none of it, and we had a stand-off at the top of the stairs. I knew that the next one who spoke would lose, so I just stared her down. My gosh, she was *so* dreadful, but I won that battle.

Next, Carol asked about the diet we were feeding Serenity. I assured her that our meals were homemade and healthy, and that Serenity was enjoying solid food.

Attempting to remain upbeat, I joked, "She really is a meat and fruit lover. My husband says that Serenity has a ten-dollar-a-day berry habit."

Carol objected abruptly. "I am not okay with that," she said, not picking up on my humour at all, and launched into a diatribe on the perils of an unbalanced diet.

Suddenly, I'd had enough. The three-part irony of this insufferable pencil-pusher questioning me on the meals I fed our infant was lost on her. First of all, I was a food blogger and had already written *LunchBox Love*, my cookbook on healthy recipes for kids that had become a national bestseller within two weeks. Second, I regularly taught classes on healthy eating and food prep at several local organic grocery stores.

And third, as I sweetly but firmly pointed out, "Ummm...actually the last time I popped into your office you were eating McDonald's takeout, and judging by your wastebasket it is a regular occurrence. So, with all due respect, I will not be taking nutrition advice from you."

It was kind of like trying to tell Jamie Oliver how to poach an egg. This was my arena, and she was questioning *me* on an unbalanced diet? Stay in your lane, Carol. Stay in your lane!

After Carol left, I phoned her boss. "I need a new worker," I said.

The situation was already so incredibly stressful that the last thing we needed was this vicious human invading our world every month with her toxic judgement. I would not have her in our home again.

WOLF IN SHEEP'S CLOTHING

Unfortunately, our next caseworker was a wolf in sheep's clothing. 'Lydia' was attentive and pleasant at first, engaging with Serenity and giving the impression that she actually cared about us and about Serenity's well-being. It was such a refreshing change that her friendly advances were welcomed and reciprocated. Lydia asked about the paint colours in our home and I happily helped her pick out paint colours for her own new home.

Her friendship, however, had barbed wire strings. It became apparent after a few visits, that our worker's support was contingent upon absolute and unquestioning compliance. As long as we agreed with everything Lydia said, there were no issues, but God help us if we disagreed with her. And of course, I did.

The second I didn't do exactly what she wanted, she chewed me up and spit me out. The price we paid for having a difference of opinion was harsh and final. As the months progressed, we received zero support from Lydia, and worse, she grew impatient with us, issuing unreasonable demands.

ALL I WANT FOR CHRISTMAS

D-day occurred two weeks before Christmas. Let's set up the scene: Serenity's MRSA was flaring alarmingly, and she had ghastly boils all over her body. I was traveling back and forth to the children's hospital twice a week with Serenity to have these boils lanced—a grisly and painful experience that was nothing short of horrifying.

Most nights I was up with Serenity because she was in so much pain. During the day I homeschooled our two young boys and, for two weeks at a time, Murray worked out of town at the oil sands north of Fort McMurray.

I was exhausted, sleep-deprived, stressed and scared. As I worried day and night for our defenseless little girl, an additional fear clawed my conscious mind: two families in our acquaintance had children who had died from MRSA complications.

In those previous several weeks there had been little opportunity for me, even for rest. It was during this dreadful stretch when I received an imperious phone call from Lydia informing me that I had until January to submit my coursework so she could complete her Home Assessment Report. The coursework she referred to were mandatory training requirements for foster and adoptive parents from the Alberta Government.

Attempting to appeal to her compassion, I told Lydia, "I don't have the time or energy right now to deal with courses. I am just trying to keep Serenity alive."

She did not ask what was going on or what they could do to help. She never asked how Serenity was doing. She never asked how I was managing under the circumstances. Instead, she scolded me like a delinquent middleschooler for not completing the courses, and began to recite the rules over the phone.

"In order to be a foster parent in the Province of Alberta, you are required by law to do this coursework."

"I just can't right now," I tried again. "I am maxed."

I finally explained to Lydia what was going on, but my attempt fell on deaf ears. Clearly there was no point in trying to negotiate an extension. I knew she wasn't listening and didn't care. Apparently, sick babies be damned. She did not care at all that I was exhausted and stretched beyond my limits. Lydia had power and enjoyed wielding it.

Unsympathetic and reproachful, she hurled her trump card.

"Well, you are expected to do it!" she all but shouted "We are paying you, after all, to foster Serenity."

And that is when I lost my shit.

HELL HATH NO FURY

"For starters," I countered, "I am currently dealing 24/7 with a health crisis for this child, and what you are paying for support, amounts to about fifty cents an hour. So, trust me, for all the work I am doing, I am extremely underpaid."

"If you don't take these courses by the deadline," she threatened. "I guess we can just remove Serenity from your home."

I nearly had an aneurysm. I'd had enough! If this bureaucratic paper-pusher was going to manipulate me with threats, she would get a dose of her own. Murray always says two things about me: "Hell hath no fury like a Mumma whose baby is mistreated," and "Sally does better research than the FBI."

If backed into a corner or told I cannot do something, my response is always to come out swinging. Challenge accepted! Prepare to be wrong.

Ok let's be honest, I probably don't speak so politely, and I may or may not raise my voice and lose my mind. Sometimes my prenatal exposure and my distinct lack of a filter is a bonus.

"Then get in your car and come get her," I shot back. "But if you do, you had better be prepared to appear on the six o'clock news. And you'd better be prepared to be unemployed, because I will bury you!" I assured Lydia that I would make certain she was the most hated person in the province.

"Game on!" I told her, "I promise you, I will win," and I hung up on her. I did not have the strength to maintain my bravado any further.

I sobbed for half an hour and then I got up and closed the blinds. I told my boys, "Do not answer the door. Ever. Even if it is the police. Just pretend we are not home."

The boys, aged eleven and thirteen at the time, were well aware of the volatile situation. They readily agreed.

Now my husband, who is normally calm and level-headed, was livid when I phoned him an hour later.

"I will call her, and I will deal with this," he said.

Lydia gushed sweetly to Murray, expressing how sorry she was for upsetting me. She assured him that she would call me immediately to work this all out and make it right.

This was a lie. She did not call immediately. Lydia was preparing her attack. When she finally called two days later it was with her supervisor, 'Cathy,' on the line. Together Lydia and Cathy tag-teamed an abusive onslaught for the next thirty minutes. They wouldn't let me speak; they wouldn't let me explain. They reprimanded me like a delinquent child, and I was punished accordingly.

In their inhumane ignorance and utter lack of compassion for a sweet little girl who was desperately ill and in pain, those two dragons perpetuated the abuse they were supposed to be protecting her from.

I was dying inside, and they kicked me like a dog. It was truly my darkest hour, and as I cried angry tears, I did not know how I would continue breathing if they took our baby away. I was beaten down and so scared that I agreed to everything they said. The biggest joke of this was that Lydia was supposed to be Murray's and my support worker.

OK, WHAT THE HELL IS GOING ON?

Three days later I was forced to welcome Lydia back into our home with Serenity's caseworker, 'Karen.' (That is not her real name, either, but 'Karen' was one of the few good ones.) The meeting was arranged to discuss steps going forward.

Swallowing my tears, I primed for war and I prepared a lovely lunch for them. During the meal I peppered Serenity's worker with pointed questions regarding reasons they might remove a child from a foster home. Karen was confused by the inquisition, but I was saccharine-sweet, and she helpfully listed all the infractions that would constitute grounds for removal. I had committed none of those offenses—not even close, but I was making a point. I was letting our support worker know, in no uncertain terms, that I was not going to be bullied and that she had better back off. No one was going to take Serenity.

Unable to handle the awkwardness any longer, Lydia made her excuses and departed, thank God!

As soon as Lydia left, Karen turned to me and said, "What the hell is going on?"

I outlined the whole grisly story. Karen was outraged.

"Listen, when it comes to Serenity, I am God," she said. "I am the one who decides where she goes and does not go. If Lydia had come and grabbed her away, I would have been notified immediately. I would have gone and got her and put her right back in your home. Your support worker has no right to threaten that."

Relief and validation flooded me. It was in that moment that I once again resolved to never let anyone take my power away.

I KNEW YOU WERE GOING TO BE DIFFICULT

Murray returned home from his work shift and immediately called to demand an appointment with 'Julie' (not her real name), the Children's Services manager in our division. Our meeting with her might have been the hardest two hours of my life.

Rather than acknowledging that our situation with Serenity's health was uniquely stressful and demanding, Julie refused to compromise on what she apparently considered to be unbreakable rules—namely completing the coursework by the January deadline. Instead of initiating a rational discussion of workable solutions, she subjected Murray and I to further rebuke for failing to comply with these expected requirements, regardless of Serenity's extenuating health situation.

"Wow. Just. Wow," was all I could say at the manager's utter lack of empathy.

Evidently placing a child in a good and loving home was not the primary goal at all. It was to establish their imperial role of God in the lives of those children and the families they were hired to support. This was such a rampant theme, that a few social workers actually admitted to me, "Sally, it is never really about the child."

I asked Julie, "How can you not look at this foster home as a win and say, 'These people love their daughter beyond words; they will fight to the death for her?'"

Julie huffed, "I knew you were going to be difficult." Then she scolded me for using 'too strong of language.'

No, I didn't drop the 'f bomb,' as one who knows me might assume. My offense was having the audacity to refer to Serenity as "our daughter."

I was furious. "I think your controlling power-trip is disgusting," I told her.

She glared silently, but her annoyed expression said, *Oh, this one is going to challenge us. This one cannot be controlled.* And she couldn't have been more right.

VINDICATION AND VALIDATION

One bright note of that office showdown however, was that since we informed Julie that we would be seeking legal advice and were considering going to the media, I was afforded the right to confront the two vile women who had called and threatened me.

In the presence of their manager, I let the women have it with both barrels. And they had to sit there, mouths shut, and listen to me denounce their unprofessional behaviour and outline all the rules Lydia had broken. I didn't pull any punches. I told them exactly what I thought of them and how badly they had damaged me.

It was a hollow vindication. As my husband and I left the meeting, my head pounding from a migraine, Murray told them we would think about how we planned to move forward. Frankly, we were just humouring them to get me the hell out of there. It was patently evident that we could no longer deal with this office and needed to be moved.

Later that afternoon Murray phoned Julie back and informed her we had made the decision that we could not work with their office any further. He said she would need to move us, effective immediately.

For the moment, it felt as though the power had been restored to the ones who truly cared. Hell hath no fury like a mother scorned, and a mother to Serenity I was, regardless of the legalities.

We were transferred to another office and assigned a new support worker. 'Derek' was an older gentleman who had kids and a beating heart. He came forewarned of how *difficult* I was, so he couldn't have been more surprised at our first home visit. He walked around the house with a bemused expression on his face as though something didn't quite add up. Finally sitting down, Derek began to ask questions about what happened with the previous support worker—from my perspective. He listened carefully, shaking his head. He seemed absolutely shocked.

"Why would anyone in their right mind take this child away from this home? I do not understand. This makes no sense!"

Then as if dismissing it as nonsense, he went on, "Okay, let's talk about the MRSA. I did a little research before I came and I have seen how dangerous this is. This particular bug lives on hard surfaces for three months. You're going to need help. What can we do to help you here at home?"

As if to back up his words, he phoned his supervisor while still sitting there, and ordered a cleaning lady for us for ten hours a week.

Derek was a rare breed: a support worker who was actually a caring human being. Sadly, he was injured in an accident not long after, and we were transferred to yet another office for the adoption to be finalized.

And then more hell ensued.

VICTIMS OF THE SYSTEM

To be fair, Serenity's adoption worker resolutely worked to obtain a permanent guardian order. 'Louanne' knew Serenity was best placed with us and wanted to accomplish that for us, but she had a huge mountain to climb.

The system is flawed and broken, and it does little to meet the vast needs of the children they are supposed to protect. More frequently it causes more damage than it benefits. We have to find a better way. Our kids in foster care need us to *care* enough about them to *actually* help them. They need someone to put their needs first and check egos at the door. They all deserve a Mum like me to fight to the death for them.

Once Serenity was transferred to the adoption's office, we faced the substantial hurdle of tired and complacent social workers. Part of the complication in Alberta with adopting Indigenous children in foster care is the considerable control that the Bands have over their children. Adoption into non-Indigenous families is a complex process. The Bands consent to children and youth to be fostered, yet they grant zero rights or authority over how they should be raised.

Before an Indigenous child can be adopted, his or her Band must endorse and sign off on the adoption. Several factors are involved in approving the adoption of an Indigenous child. One of those requirements included writing an Indigenous Plan. In our plan, we outlined the ways in which we would ensure Serenity remembered her Indigenous culture and heritage.

Pointing out that Serenity was only one-quarter Native, I asked our worker, "What about her other racial heritage? She is half Caucasian and one-quarter Filipino as well."

Louanne said dismissively, "Doesn't matter. It's only the Native part that counts."

I beg to disagree. Either *all* of her heritage matters, or *none* of it does. Her Indigenous culture is valuable and important, but we are focusing on the wrong thing.

As a foster kid in the system who has lived it, I can tell you kids don't care about that. All I cared about was a mum and a dad and a feeling of belonging. Mandating that Serenity—a child with extreme sensory auditory processing disorder—must attend an Indigenous round dance with loud chanting and beating drums was nothing short of cruel. Was her one-quarter Indigenous culture so all-important that it superseded her trauma and hurt brain? The fallout of that event left Serenity so traumatized and terrified that for days after she clung to me like glue.

NO ONE SHOWED UP

During this time, however, I had discovered that the government retained the power to overrule a Band if it is deemed in the best interest of the child to be adopted. (This has since been reverted back to granting the Bands full authority.) As one who traversed adoption through the foster system, let me assert it is always in the best interest of the child to be adopted and to carry the name of their adopted parents to truly feel part of the family.

We fondly referred to our adoption worker, Louanne, as Eeyore. She was friendly enough, but she moped slowly along and was often absent with sick days. I developed a dance between encouragingly stroking her ego and anxiously pushing her to get the damn job done. It was painstaking. Louanne would report that she had attempted to contact the Band, but they would not call her back so she couldn't get them to sign off on the paperwork. This went on for months.

After enduring a year of these delays, I said at last, "Enough is enough! I want to go in front of the Government Board to have the Band overruled."

Louanne agreed to write a report for the board and to attend the hearing. Our relief that we were finally making progress and moving forward was short-lived when I received a call from Louanne a few weeks later. She was scheduled for surgery the same date as the hearing and therefore wouldn't be available to attend.

I eagerly offered to go in her place, but she said that's not how it worked, and she was not allowed to let me go. I phoned her supervisor and begged. *No,* the supervisor reiterated, I could not go, but she promised that someone from their office would represent Serenity, swearing to me that if necessary, she would go herself.

On the date of the board hearing, no one showed up to represent Serenity.

Not one!

Our petition was denied. I was livid when I learned of their incompetence. One of the board members, an Indigenous Elder, asked questions regarding visitation. He was particularly interested in allowing visits with the child's grandparents. If I had been allowed to go, I could have simply explained that such visitations were impossible and irrelevant, because both grandparents were dead. Since no one was present as an agent for Serenity, his unanswered question caused the board to reject overruling the Band.

When we learned of the board's decision, we were on holiday in the United States. We had already dealt with an incredibly frustrating situation caused by Eeyore, because she had neglected to obtain the necessary letter of permission from the director so that our family could travel out of the country with Serenity. She had forgotten, so the paperwork was delayed. I'd already had to raise hell to receive the permission letter in time for us to fly out on the holiday. And here we were receiving a long-distance call to inform us that our petition was denied by the board because no one had appeared to represent the child they promised to protect.

A flurry of expensive long-distance calls were made to the Alberta Office of the Child and Youth Advocate to report the negligence of our children's services office. For once, the advocate we were assigned was understanding and efficient. He assured us that we had a solid case and he immediately filed a report. Abruptly, our adoption office was scrambling because—although they would never admit it—they knew they had screwed up.

CONSIDER YOURSELVES LUCKY

Isn't it peculiar that for a full year Louanne could not reach the Band, yet as soon as I called in an advocate, within twenty-four hours he'd expediently contacted the Band? In an unexpected turn of events, not only was the Band willing to support and sign off on Serenity's adoption, they extended an invitation to Driftpile Cree Nation (Serenity's Band) for a Memorial Round Dance and ceremony to bless her adoption.

Rather than admit their mistake and appropriately apologize for any delinquent actions, the workers from our child services office acted like proud conquering heroes. I'd had to do all the damn work. I'd had to push and kick and scream to get them to do their job, but they were the heroes that made it happen. *Really?* Every step of the way they let Serenity down. When her adoption was officially granted, we were told that we should consider ourselves lucky because it was the fastest adoption their office had ever had. "The fastest adoption?"

I wanted to scream, "It took three bloody years!"

Shame on you all, I thought. The only reason that the adoption went through at all was because I was such an aggressive bitch. I am okay with that title, by the way. I have a deep desire to have no lasting sorrow or regret, no stone unturned, and no if-onlys. All along I have always said that if these women liked me then I needed to have a good hard look at myself, because there was a fatal flaw in my character.

Judgement has been rampant in all of this, but to be crystal clear, none of the problems and stress emanated from Serenity herself. That wee girl is a breath of fresh air, funny and sweet and so incredibly smart that most days she blows our minds with the intelligence that springs from her little mind.

CHAPTER 5

Meeting Birth Families

Whoever says that blood is thicker than water, hasn't met my family, yet.
~ UNKNOWN

IT IS INEVITABLE THAT AN ADOPTED PERSON will one day want to meet their birth mother and her family. Honestly, in most of the experiences that adoptees have shared with me, after their initial excitement and happiness of finding birth families, they found that trying to maintain an ongoing relationship ended up being awkward and disappointing.

There are no set rules. It is such uncharted territory. What do you call them? Do you call them by their first names? Aunt? Mum? And if adoptive parents are still in the picture, you worry about offending or hurting feelings. Often guilt or a sense of being disloyal leads adoptees to wait into adulthood to meet their birth family.

FINDING MY BIO FAMILY

The search for my birth mother is a two-part story. Part one started when I was eighteen, after Mum died and my dad was dissolving into alcoholic oblivion. Life at home had collapsed around me and my feelings of not belonging overwhelmed me. With no one's feelings left to hurt, I decided that I wanted to search for my birth mother. I prayed secretly that I would find her because, in my head, I believed this was where I would finally belong. I would find my tribe.

I went through the normal channels and registered on the Alberta Post Adoption Registry, but accessing the documents I needed, proved to be far more difficult than I'd anticipated. My birth mother was not on the registry, nor any of my birth family, so I was only given some non-identifying scraps of information like my birth name and where I was born. (Not so conveniently, the hospital where I'd been born in Calgary had been destroyed only five years before.) None of the information was very useful.

It was ironic and frustrating that all rights belonged to my birth mother. Even though the adoption was supposedly for 'my benefit,' what a joke that was. I was the one with zero rights. The adoptee is the last person considered in the whole equation and it infuriated me.

At the time, I thought: *She's the one that made the 'mistake,' but the laws protect her. How does that work? What about me? I didn't ask to be brought here. This was her doing, so how does she end up holding all the cards?*

With no choice but to give up, it was ten years before part two of the search for my birth mother began again.

Just before I got married, I hired a private investigator. In the meantime, I was told by the registry that supposedly the records had been opened, which I might add was a joke. They would not release to me any more actual information unless I hired the registry's so-called investigator at a huge cost. Why did I have to pay for my own information? Their investigator was incompetent and had absolutely no investigative skills to find anyone. But without my birth mother's identifying details, my own private investigator hit another dead-end.

I eventually negotiated a collaboration with my PI. Miraculously, within the hour, she had located my birth mother. However, the registry continued to hold me hostage for that information until I paid the $750 ransom. I didn't. I wouldn't.

Disgusted by the treatment I was given by the government agent, my PI called and told me she could not live with herself knowing she had the information that I had so desperately tried to track down. She facilitated the meeting with my birth mother.

HIGH HOPES AND BIG DISAPPOINTMENTS

It was not until I was in my thirties that I finally met my birth mother. I really thought it was the ticket, that I would feel connected and *finally* be part of something. I could not have been more wrong. Even though connected biologically, I was still part of nothing.

In the beginning, I was thrilled to finally have the opportunity to meet her—my bio mother—and it was a relief to learn where I had inherited some of my traits like my height and fair skin. But as time passed, and the novelty wore off, I began to feel like she only tolerated me and found me annoying. I was a complete enigma to her, and she didn't quite know what to do with me. I suspect she didn't really want me around. I tried, but the relationship did not work. She thought we were going to play happy families, but although I had wanted so badly to connect, I simply could not continue the effort. She was a broken and damaged woman when she neglected me as an infant, and she was still too broken for me to ever fit in with her life, because clearly, I did not, and never had.

Adopted children want to please, so it is troubling when we don't. Reunification is a complicated and hard process, but luckily, I have been blessed to have an extended birth family aside from my biological mother, who have welcomed me and my family with open arms. Even though they are lovely people who treat me kindly, sometimes at family gatherings I feel like a ghost circling, floating above, seeing what is going on, but not part of it.

Environmental upbringing really does matter. I had been raised in a household that was poles apart, with completely different values than my biological mother. Among the lessons that my amazing adoptive mum taught me was to embrace being different, follow my own ideas, and do what I think is right. She never wanted me to follow the crowd, ever.

In a lot of ways, I love that about myself, but it can be a lonely existence. The life I had created with Murray and our children was polar opposite to my bio mother. I no longer have any connection with her whatsoever. There remains a lingering heaviness that I cannot define. Meeting her did not fill the hole that I was convinced it would. It didn't change anything. Apparently, it wasn't someone else's job to fill the hole, I had to do the work myself.

TELL HER SHE IS ADOPTED

People often wonder if they should tell their child they are adopted. *Ok, seriously?* I can't even believe that I have to address this question.

In case you are wondering—*yes*, you have to tell them they are adopted!

Here is the thing: lies and omissions will always come out. Great Aunt Martha may let it slip in her old age. Some kid at school will blurt out the whispers he overheard from his parents. A medical issue will crop up that requires an explanation. Yes, you have to tell them, and the sooner the better. In my opinion, the key is to not make a federal issue of it. Don't sit down and have 'the chat.' Conversations should be as normal as passing the salt, incorporated all the time in little daily things. Let children know at age appropriate times and seriously, the less big deal you make of it the better.

One evening when I was twelve, I asked Mum a question about my life before the adoption. From my chair at the kitchen table, I could clearly see her reflection in the window above the kitchen sink, dishes clinking as she washed, and her reaction at my innocent words.

"Mum," I asked naively, "What was my birth name before I was adopted?"

Head lowered and hands stilled in the sink, Mum literally froze. I saw in that split second, abject fear flicker across her face. Though she kept her head turned away, I saw her reflection betray the flood of emotions. With a suppressed sigh of resignation, she answered me, but that moment seared in my brain: *Do not ask questions!*

Honestly, I think she felt threatened. Which is why, decades later, when Serenity asked me why her skin was so much darker than mine, I remembered that encounter with my mum, and I did not hesitate or skip a beat. I explained that she was part Indigenous because her mother was half Indigenous and half Filipino. We talked for a moment about how Filipino people have darker skin. She thought this through and nodded. No big chat, no federal case. I gave a straight answer, and with it the freedom to know that if she had more questions they would be answered.

WE NEED TO KNOW WHERE WE COME FROM

When you are adopted, no matter how loved and supported you are, there is always a piece missing. It makes us think differently, feel differently. We have a harder time figuring people out. We need deeper, more meaningful relationships. We don't do superficial.

An adoptee really does need to know where they came from, no matter how good or bad. We just need to fit that puzzle piece that is missing. It is essential. Adoptive parents do not need to get all weird and freak out, thinking they are losing their child. *Newsflash*, this is not about you! The mum and dad who raised me will always be my parents. They are my heart and I will love them forever, but knowing how I came to this earth is equally important. It is a longing that must be fulfilled.

But here is my opinion on open adoptions—and I feel strongly about it. They are not a good thing. Children do not have the emotional maturity to handle an open adoption. There are so many unpredictable variables and it often proves to be confusing and distressing for the child.

Open adoptions may look different in various circumstances, depending on the boundaries stipulated by all parties (except the child), but essentially it is a concept where the birth mother and adoptive family have a continued relationship, and the birth mother retains connection with her child throughout their life. While this seems good in theory, my experience has been that the relationship ends up confusing with no one being clear on their true roles. The loser is the child. *Always.*

My advice as an adoptive parent, is to obtain as much information as possible about your child's bio parent(s) and when you feel it is best, provide it on a need-to-know basis. I promise you, though, when they are grown up, they will want to know more and to meet their bio parent if the opportunity is there. While they are children, however, it may be wise to distance that relationship.

My daughter did not come from a good place. Apprehended at only a few weeks old from a crack den, her tiny body was coursing with the byproducts of her mother's alcohol, heroin, and crystal meth addiction. In spite of repeated attempts, Serenity's birth mother has never been able to get clean or have any kind of life that would be safe for the several children she has birthed and been forced to say goodbye to. I have pictures of Serenity's birth mother and father, and I know their names, but for Serenity's protection, she will not have access to that information until she is old enough to understand what happened.

When a child is curious in their teens the reasons are very different than in adulthood. In adulthood, the inquiry is mature and logical, and perhaps even prompted by a need for medical background. A pissed off teenager in search of their birth parent is a recipe for disaster, and the grass will always look greener on the other side.

No matter how we try to normalize adoption, you need to be clear on the fact that adopted kids *are* different. We all have identity issues, so knowing who we are and where we come from is incredibly important. When a child's race or heritage differs from her adoptive family, as Serenity's does, identity issues can be complicated, and can't be discounted by pretending that the elephant is not in the room. Trust me, the more you ignore it, the worse it is.

Adoption is special and such an amazing gift, but if you behave like it is a dirty little secret that no one talks about, it makes us feel that there is something wrong with us. I cannot stress it enough: what we hide becomes *wrong* in the eyes of a child. Make adoption a normal topic of conversation, and when your child is ready and wants to talk, they will know it's a safe subject.

CHAPTER 6

FASD is not a Four-Letter Word

Some days I amaze myself; other days I look for my phone while I'm holding it.
~ EVERY WOMAN, Everywhere

✳ ✳ ✳

FOR MANY FAMILIES, taking on the commitment of raising a foster child is incredibly daunting. They hear horror stories of coping with a myriad of health consequences from behavioural to developmental. Among the most feared 'dirty words' is FASD (Fetal Alcohol Spectrum Disorder).

When Serenity first came to us, we knew that an infant apprehended from a drug den had zero chance of bypassing the inevitable neurological consequences. I immediately began scouring the internet, but it yielded absolutely nothing about healing a child from FASD. The common misconception is that these children are born with holes in their brain. The material I found only focused on symptoms and what behaviours to expect.

I naively asked myself, Before Sir Frederick Banting discovered insulin, people with Type 1 Diabetes would die. In the early 1900s, one in four children died of an infection before Sir Alexander Fleming discovered antibiotics by accident in 1921. So why can't I just find the solution to help Serenity that hasn't been discovered yet?

Right then I knew I was about to invent a new wheel. If I wanted my child to have an opportunity to thrive and have an amazing life. I knew I was going to have to do hard things. I had already done a boatload of hard things. What made this any different? I knew then, and even now that I have naysayers, but how could I tell Serenity that she didn't deserve my effort? How could I sleep at night if I gave up before I even tried? I would stand up for her and I would fight for her.

My search began hardcore. I dug deep for the kind of help and answers we needed. I read books to understand how the brain works and the effect of drugs and alcohol upon it. I read everything I could find and searched out courses and seminars. I enmeshed myself into the job of helping my daughter, informing myself on anything that could facilitate change in Serenity's life. And I gathered ammunition against the naysayers—anything to get rid of defeatism and breathe in hope.

FASD WORKSHOPS AND SO-CALLED EXPERTS

Not all the courses I found had the same value. One FASD workshop I attended featured "the FASD expert" in our area as one of the guest speakers. Everyone had ranted about this woman and I was excited to go, certain that I would leave with some excellent strategies. I was not alone in this desperate hope.

During the lunch break I spoke to a man who admitted to me that he and his wife were at their wits end.

"What is our limit?" he asked me. His face was lined with worry and his shoulders drooped in defeat. I know he felt like a failure and that they were hanging on by a thread.

"Where is the end of the rope?" he shook his head.

And then the eagerly awaited "expert" came out to speak after lunch.

The first words out of her mouth were, "Anything you think you know about Fetal Alcohol Spectrum Disorder, throw it out! You know nothing." I kid you not.

Just as her startled audience was processing this pronouncement, she issued her next statement with ominous finality.

"The best you can hope for is to keep them out of jail, and if your child is a girl, put her on the pill or you will be raising your grandchild."

I felt sickened at her damning words. I thought of the man I'd spoken with during the break and could only imagine how devastated he must have felt. I could have cried for him and his wife. I would not have been surprised if he went out to his car after the seminar and called his social worker to come pick up the kids. They were done. I was heartsick for him.

Seriously? That was supposed to be inspiring? My bullshit meter shot off the charts. It was pretty clear to me that our so-called expert was just trying to capitalize off of heartbroken and exhausted parents to promote her consulting business. Her pitch was intended to scare the crowd into hiring her services to help navigate social services for more money and supports like Respite Care. I wanted to walk up to the podium and throat punch her!

When another seminar became available, I was wary. This time, the guest speaker was touted as the "foremost authority" on FASD. With so many experts, surely one of them had practical therapies for kids with prenatal exposure to drugs and alcohol?

Jeff Noble was funny and interesting, and unlike the previous woman, he was fabulous at explaining how FASD brains are different. Jeff made several great suggestions on how to handle situations, and even offered some good tools to use. But in spite of his increased level of understanding, his tagline was *FASD is forever; frustration is not.* He also cautioned that a person with FASD can't be changed, can't be healed, and won't amount to much.

When babies are exposed to drugs and alcohol in the womb, their bodies are unable to process or metabolize it. The resulting neurological damage to their central nervous system is a spectrum from serious to devastating (CDC, 2020).

I learned that among many potential behavioural and developmental consequences of FASD a child could have:

- poor memory and attention span
- learning disabilities
- hearing or vision problems
- small head, low body weight and small size
- poor coordination
- weakened heart, kidneys and bones
- distinctive ridge between nose and upper lip
- speech and language delays
- low IQ
- hyperactivity
- attention deficit disorder
- poor reasoning and judgement
- diminished conscience
- poor communication
- difficulty getting along with others
- impulsive and destructive behaviours

THAT KID WAS ME!

As I sat in that seminar listening for ways to help Serenity, it suddenly hit me. Like a tidal wave. It all made sense. I understood—*finally*—why life was so very hard for me. Why I am the way I am. Why I react the way I do. Hot tears welled up and an overwhelming urge to cry engulfed me. I hurried out of the seminar and huddled in the ladies' room, sobbing for that unhappy little girl with a lightning temper and no self-control. That emotional hot mess who was unpopular and so very misunderstood. I cried for that little girl whose brain was forever changed by prenatal exposure to alcohol, never to be the same again.

When I could finally gasp a breath, I called my husband at work.

"Murray," I cried. "That kid was me! I have FASD!"

He calmly replied, "I know, honey," in his classic, cool-headed Murray style.

I had never made the connection before, but I had always known something was wrong. Suddenly it made sense! They said I was a spoiled brat, but I was really just a little girl who was unable to handle the big, noisy, busy world around me. To say that I often acted badly was the understatement of the century, but now I knew it was because that little girl simply couldn't cope. I was not like others. I didn't know how to play nice, even though I so wanted to. I'd hated myself. Hated the way I handled situations and people. Always feeling bad afterward, I lived with regret. It wasn't fair and it wasn't my fault.

I sat and cried for that disliked and misunderstood little girl who could never seem to control her FASD-fueled behaviours and emotions. I so desperately wished that someone had known to look a little deeper. But without the research we have now, how were my adoptive parents to know? They just raised their kids the same way their parents did, and sadly it did not apply to me. I knew then that somehow, I had to use my own experiences to help change the conversation around FASD.

FASD IN THE CLASSROOM

I do not believe that labelling a child is productive. At best, it gives educators and parents a place to start. At worst it erodes belief, expectation and hope. FASD in the classroom is a destructive label waiting to happen. So here is the problem with putting a child with a hurt brain in a school setting. They are set up to fail. When these kids are struggling the most, they act up and behave badly. And typically, they find themselves in the crosshairs of a teachers' disciplinary action. All manner of labels follow them for the rest of their lives, and not in a good way.

Even without the FASD diagnosis, I had my own share of labels. I *hated* school. Every single minute of it. I hated the noisy, crowded hallways, the other kids, and the teachers who didn't like me, either. I couldn't understand my schoolwork and I felt stupid. I imagine I was too hyper, because I couldn't sit still, and I could not stop talking. I vividly remember the daily humiliation of school. It was absolute torture for me.

What is interesting for me now, and something that I didn't piece together until I discovered my own link to FASD, is that I *still* can't sit for extended periods of time. All-day classes or seminars are excruciating. I really struggle to stay focused and sit still. I have learned though, to be kind to myself and accept that this is who I am. I have learned to not set myself up for failure and pain. No matter how interesting the workshop, I am careful to not book myself into all-day sessions that require me to sit for long hours. I need to get up and take breaks.

I do the same for my daughter. Guarding her surroundings very closely has become instinctual. I am cognizant of not putting her in situations that she cannot handle, in ways I always wished had been done for me. For example, I give her a pass on stressful, noisy settings like the kids' church we tried and abandoned because it was simply too loud and chaotic for her.

It is one of the main reasons why we chose to homeschool her. It was obvious from the beginning that for Serenity, the traditional school environment would have been an academic disaster. School at home has been a game-changer. We read, we play math games, we do science experiments. We bake and do crafts and then we read some more. Whenever I see Serenity starting to squirm, we change it up and go do something fun. We jump up, take a break, and get our wiggles out. Whatever work she has completed for that particular subject is done, no matter where we are. Homeschooling takes the social stress out of her life. She learns at her own pace and takes breaks when she needs it. She can grow and develop in a safe and nurturing setting with no pressure to fit into a box that will clearly never fit. Instead of torture, Serenity's learning has been positive, successful and *real*.

CHOOSING TO AIM HIGHER

The current paradigm taught by child welfare is unhelpful, antiquated, and hopeless. It does nothing to equip parents with the necessary tools to handle a child with FASD. Even most FASD educators only burden parents with what they are up against. They give little hope of making any sort of difference for their child let alone a chance to succeed. Their advice to just "get through it," leaves parents to helplessly let the chips fall where they may and the best that they can hope for is to keep their kids out of jail.

This is wrong on so many levels! It *must change*—for my wee girl and for others like us. I know these kids can lead full lives. For heaven's sake, look at me! Despite everything, I am a functioning member of society, a wife, a mother, an author, a blogger, and an advocate for children like me. So, there *is* hope!

Truly believing that I could make a difference, I refused to accept that I was tackling a hopeless cause. I dug in harder to seek out answers and guess what I discovered? There are other options. In a 2002 rat study, some scientists explored whether they could reverse the effects of alcohol-related brain damage using an obstacle course to teach rats a series of complicated motor skills. What they discovered was that this training seemed to develop new neural pathways in the brains of adult rats. Their experiments have encouraged neurologists and child psychologists to explore the therapeutic potential to develop the motor function of children (and adults) with FASD (Klintsova, et al, 2002).

There may not be a definitive "cure" for the FASD brain, but early diagnosis and intervention is starting to show promise with brain development using the science of neuroplasticity. (Olson and Montague, 2011). This is exciting research, but I know that neurological rehabilitation is no easy task. (Read more about it in Chapter 8: Healing Strategies.) It takes a loving home, surrounded by family that is prepared to go the distance and do whatever it takes. None of this is easy, but I can promise you, for a family dealing with FASD, the effort is worth it.

CHAPTER 7

Coping with the Aftermath

I have learned two very important things in my life.
I can't remember the first one, but the second one is to write everything down.
~ UNKNOWN

LIKE EVERY ADOPTEE, both Serenity's and my adoption stories are lifelong experiences that affect us uniquely. We will inevitably struggle with adoption-related issues throughout our lives, regardless of how positive or negative the circumstances were.

As a child, I always felt different, unheard and misunderstood. I never really knew who I was, and I felt like no one cared what I was thinking or what I wanted. I often felt invisible except when I became volatile and acted out. I believe that the fallout of my early experiences and wounds defined who I was and who I became. For me, the uncertainty of my entry into the world, the repressed trauma from my birth mother's neglect, the bullying from my brother and other kids, and living in the constant terror of my abusive uncle, all had their own degree of impact upon me.

UNICORNS AND HAPPY ENDINGS?

Hollywood's version of adoption with rainbows, unicorns and happy endings is not reality. Here's the deal. When a family receives their adorable baby for adoption, or when the process is officially stamped *final*, this is not the beginning. The beginning was that the child came to them through trauma. Their new family was built on the foundation of enormous loss—loss of their first mother, their first family, their history, their connection to the world, and perhaps even their name.

Please do not minimize it by pretending it doesn't exist. Everyone involved is dealing with an intense experience and these conflicting emotions set them up for unrealistic expectations. Adoption is loss, and it forms who we are. Anger, denial, anxiety and fear are all part of the grief felt by adopted children. I felt them all. They manifested in behaviour problems, fear of rejection and abandonment, unhealthy relationships, and broken friendships.

Not long ago, a friend who had adopted a little girl shared that her daughter had flipped out after school when she couldn't find her mum. My friend seemed puzzled by the outburst.

"She was doing so good; I don't understand," She said. My friend did not recognize that her daughter's intense reaction was fear of abandonment, not bad behaviour. Adoption makes us vulnerable. It is a consequence of loss. We don't come to you at ground zero; we come at minus fifty. You have to deal with that before you are even out of the gate. Don't judge us as 'doing good' or 'doing bad.' What we need is reassurance for our insecurities. Teach us to accept and embrace who we are—that we are enough—that how we came into this world is irrelevant. Tell us for the eight-millionth time that you love us and will never abandon us, because we need it. We crave it.

Even when Murray and I were first married, if he hung up the telephone without saying he loved me, I would be so worried and upset. Adopted and foster kids need to be reminded and reassured all the time that we are loved.

WORDS ARE NOT ENOUGH

One December when Serenity had been with us for five years and adopted legally for three, we were baking Christmas cakes. My mum had a tradition where we would make a wish over the batter. As we did this, Serenity's wish was that *Mummy would love her forever.* I nearly started sobbing!

I cherish that little girl so much and work daily to make her feel safe and loved, yet hardwired into her nature, she needed more. Well, let me tell you darling girl, my solemn promise to you is *wish granted.* I will love you forever!

Understand one fundamental truth: words are not enough to erase the effects of the trauma! It is stronger and more powerful than we realize. It is always there, because pain that is buried alive, never dies. At some point, therapy is essential for foster kids and adoptees to come to terms with their painful emotions, but more importantly to understand who they are.

Only now, as an adult, have I begun to deal with the loss in my own life, but it has made a huge difference. So many of the issues that we face stem from not knowing who we are. We come from two worlds, yet we fit in neither.

I couldn't do this alone. I needed a team. During my life I have seen more than a dozen therapists, but frankly they were all rubbish, and that is being generous. One disastrous session after another left me shaken and re-traumatized from dredging up the shitshow of my past and leaving me to wallow in it. Not until I discovered the one therapist in all my years that was any good, did I realize that what I needed was someone to weigh-in objectively on my issues. What I needed was *practical* help to address what I came to learn was Post Traumatic Stress Disorder (PTSD). (Apparently, I scored as high in my PTSD treatment sessions as soldiers who have been through war.)

Marinating in my shit didn't change my circumstances or my feelings around them. Acknowledging that my trauma exists—and is valid—was the important piece to my healing. With the help of my amazing psychologist, Kim, I was able to move forward in my life with the knowledge that things didn't happen *to* me, they happened *for* me. I can now see the blessings in my story and perhaps even point others to their way home.

IDENTITY AND SELF ESTEEM

A second major issue for adopted children is self-esteem and the challenge of our own identity development, especially as we reach adolescence. Adoptees struggle, as I did, to find their fit in their adoptive family. There is an underlying feeling in the heart of an adoptee of being *less than*. I think of it as the Cinderella complex. We have a sense of being beholden to people, and don't ask for anything because we don't deserve it.

I already see this tendency in my daughter. Serenity never asks for anything (except blueberries). We have to pull gift ideas out of her. The hardest part of writing her Santa letter each year is that she never wants anything. The first Christmas she was old enough to understand the whole Santa gig, she asked for a pencil. I kid you not. A *pencil*. And even that was a chore to get out of her.

We had a neighbour who once asked Serenity what she wanted for her birthday and her reply was, "I am okay. I don't need anything."

The neighbour observed humorously, "I'll bet you could go outside and get a rock from the garden, wrap it up, and she would be thrilled."

Although I love that she is not entitled and demanding, there is a part of me that worries. Does she feel she cannot ask for more or that she does not deserve more? I understand, but it does make me sad.

I also felt unworthy all through my life. To this day it is still an issue for me, so I get it! I am actually more shocked when people are nice to me than I ever am when they're lousy. The lousy part is expected. Perhaps this instinct starts as a child. I mean, if your own mother can't be good to you, why would anyone else?

People thought of me as spoiled and entitled, and often told my parents exactly that, but they had no idea what was really going on in my life. This kind of misjudgment happens all the time for parents dealing with situations like ours. Recognize it for what it is, because people simply do not understand. We are all guilty of judging, but there's always a story behind the behaviour. If people really knew why we acted the way we did, they wouldn't be angry and judgmental, they would be crying.

Belonging is all anybody wants, but the feeling is elusive for one who is fostered or adopted. Not for a minute am I saying that people treat us this way. In fact, it has nothing to do with them, and everything to do with us. It is the lack of self-esteem. It is feeling different—second best. It is sitting on the periphery, looking in. No matter how many declarations we're given, adoptees struggle to fit. We often feel that we stick out like a sore thumb.

Even when a family is of the same race, like mine was, the physical differences are a glaring betrayal. I was tall and pale with blond hair and blue eyes, but my parents and adopted brother were average height and olive-skinned with dark hair and dark eyes. They seemed to tan easily by merely thinking of going outside while I, on the other hand, with the fairest skin, would be burned to a crisp in minutes at the mere mention of the sun. I always thought my brother *appeared* to belong, although if you asked him, he would probably say he didn't either.

Have you noticed that people say stupidest things? I've heard a whole litany of comments and questions that literally send me right round the twist! Seriously, resist the urge to say things like:

Do you have any of your own children?

Where did you get her from?

Was it expensive?

Is there anything wrong with her?

Do your own kids get along with her? Do they like her?

Why did her mum give her up?

So, you couldn't have any of your own?

We notice the stares, the double-takes, and the innocent comments of little kids. "Why is your girl brown and you're not?"

Speaking as both an adoptee and an adoptive parent, it can get super annoying. The worst is when Murray and I, who are a little older than your average couple with a school age child, are confused for Serenity's grandparents.

To an adopted child, these comments are insensitive idle curiosity and they don't benefit anyone in any way. It isn't enough that we have our own demons of unworthiness, we also have to contend with narrow-minded opinions, crass comments and side-long looks. And they are everywhere. Even in Superstore while shopping for tomatoes. (Yes, that really happened.)

Biology does not always dictate likeness, but it tends to deter questions of birth origin. For me, it was obvious that I was not a bio child; for my daughter, there is no escaping that we are not biological parents. Why do people put so much value on which family member we take after? For some reason people like to wrap up families in a cozy matching package and are fixated on differences in looks. They make assumptions and comments that are intended to be harmless, but sadly often end in lost innocence for the adoptee. I remember once when Graeme and I told someone that we were brother and sister and they couldn't believe it.

Awkwardly, they said, "Oh yeah, I can see where you guys look alike; it's in your eyes."

We laughed and asked, "Why? Because we both have them?"

Why do we—as a society—feel the need to make ourselves feel better by somehow looking alike? I say, *embrace the differences*. Embrace the beauty. Embrace people for who they are.

RACISM OR JUST PLAIN STUPIDITY?

When Serenity was six, she had to have extensive dental surgery under anesthetic. Typically, when children are prenatally exposed to alcohol or drugs, the enamel on their teeth is weak and they will develop severe dental issues.

That same night Serenity changed. She no longer had any interest in reading or being read to. She seemed spacy and 'not there.' It was the end of November, so I just chalked it up to her being *done* with schoolwork. We decided to take a break and reconvene after Christmas.

But nothing changed after Christmas. January went by and at the end of February, one of the teeth that had been capped became abscessed and had to be removed. Murray took Serenity for that appointment. They couldn't get her mouth frozen enough, so the dentist kept adding more and more anesthetic. After much struggle, the tooth finally came out and we thought the problems were solved. Murray brought her home and we cuddled her on the sofa all day.

Then that night, she looked at me with a glazed expression and said, "I'm blind, Mummy. I'm blind."

Within a few seconds the moment passed. I was shocked and scared by the incident, but I had no idea what Serenity had just experienced. In the moment, there seemed to be nothing I could do except sit her down and watch her closely.

The rest of the month passed with these odd episodes of being spaced out and unable to see continuing several times a day. Each time, following these ten-second episodes, she would return right back to normal and carry on with what she was doing. In retrospect, I should have been more alarmed, but the episodes were not dramatic, and they were over as quickly as they started.

Then one afternoon in March, Serenity came downstairs holding her front tooth in her hand.

"My tooth fell out, Mummy," she said, and dropped unconscious to the floor.

That night, I took her to a walk-in clinic. The doctor on-call was kind and actually took time to listen and take me seriously. Even though by this point in the evening Serenity looked like a perfectly normal little girl, the doctor proceeded to conduct a neurological exam. Believing it to be epileptic seizures, the doctor recommended that I take her to the Stollery Children's Hospital that same evening.

What he knew that I didn't, was that as Serenity became more tired, her seizures would increase; it would be evident to the pediatricians to make a clear diagnosis. He was right.

The night we were there it was like a warzone; the emergency room was full to the rafters and the sounds of puking surrounded us. As the long night progressed, Serenity's seizures became more frequent and pronounced.

The doctors and nurses were incredible with Serenity. She was swiftly placed into an examination room and scheduled for a CT scan.

Now, because Serenity's MRSA as an infant was still on her medical file, she was placed in isolation. Although she was completely healed from it, any history of a resistant bacteria remains on file forever (just like a family history of diabetes). The hospital is required to flag it and treat her like she still has it. Which, by the way, I had no problem with. Serenity had her own bathroom, and everyone was far away from us. That, in itself, was a win.

But that night there was one obnoxious scan technician who passed judgement after a mere glance at my Indigenous child, and I suspect she will regret it for a very long time.

It was three o'clock in the morning when the nurse and I arrived with Serenity for her CT scan. I knew that deep down what they were looking for was a brain tumour. Let me tell you, I was stressed. But there was no pleasant greeting for us.

As we approached, the technician yelled at the nurse, "Thanks for telling me ahead that this is an 'isolation case!'"

Apparently, they had neglected to forewarn the lab. Not an ounce of kindness was extended to an exhausted and worried mother or her terrified little girl. As the technician busied herself with setting up the machine, she abruptly stopped and turned to me.

"Do me a favour," she snarled. "Don't you touch anything. The last thing I need is to have to clean and sanitize the entire place after you leave!"

I was in shock. I was speechless, and trust me, I am never speechless. I just shot a dirty look at her back.

When she was finally ready, the technician turned again and barked at me, "Well, lift her onto the table. I am not touching her!" Her unspoken words rung in the silence: *dirty Native kid.*

Incensed, I walked over to my girl and kissed her cheek as I picked her up. I smooched her again as I placed her on the examining table. Then—now, I know this was really immature, but to this day I do regret it—looking straight at the technician, I deliberately ran my hands all over every surface I could. Standing beside me, the nurse fought back laughter; I think she was secretly cheering me on.

And that is when the technician said the words that unhinged me. She wanted Serenity to turn her head a certain way for the scan, but since she refused to touch Serenity, she barked, "Turn your head and look at —" To me and said, "What are you? Her foster Mum? Aunt? Who are you to her?"

Again, for a brief second, I was speechless. And then I was livid. "I am her mother!" I said. "And FYI, Serenity is not deaf. She can hear you. Dial back your racism!"

The scans were finished in cold silence. When the technician was done, we left the lab, the nurse apologizing profusely as she rolled Serenity back to her room.

"It's not your fault," I assured the nurse. "But I will be dealing with her later."

Back in the isolation room, settled but still afraid, Serenity asked me, "Why didn't she think you were my Mummy?" (This experience was her first real exposure to racism, and she didn't know how to process it.)

"Because she is stupid!" I quickly replied.

For Serenity, I reported the heartless technician to the head of the imaging department.

ADDRESSING THE ELEPHANT

One day, when my daughter was five years old, she finally noticed the difference in our skin colour. I knew that how I responded to this surprised discovery would set the course of her self-esteem and her feeling of belonging as an ethnic child adopted into a Caucasian home.

We were bathing and as our legs brushed close, Serenity observed, "Mummy look at how much browner my skin is to yours!"

She was kind of shocked, and I think mildly concerned. This was a pivotal moment. Not only was it time to address the elephant, I had to look it straight in the eye.

I said, "I know! Isn't it awesome? Don't we just go together so well? Look how pretty your gorgeous brown skin is next to my pale skin! Don't you just love it?"

A giant smile split her face and she said "yes." Subject over.

In that moment, we embraced our different skin colour and made it a beautiful thing. Most importantly, we didn't need to have an awkward discussion. It was in that instant, with a flash of rare insight, that I discovered it all comes down to *normalizing* the differences. Acknowledge them and move on.

On another occasion, we were driving to pick up Brady. He had been out in the sun and had a bit of a sunburn.

I said to Brady, "Sorry for giving you this pale, pasty white skin that is prone to sunburns."

Immediately, Serenity piped up. "Yeah, I got my skin from Daddy."

"Yes, baby, you sure did," I smiled.

Now, for the record, Murray's skin is as pale as mine, but you see, little kids don't see skin colour. They just see people. They just see love. And love is what makes a family, not just blood. But we seriously need to embrace the differences and let them be. How we look should not be our defining trait.

I'm not saying to ignore them or pretend they aren't there, but it isn't necessary to make a federal issue over them either. We simply don't need to make problems where there are none, and we really don't need to focus on them.

Our daughter is gorgeous and exotic; there is no way of pretending that she is biologically ours. So, let's not be silly. She may not have the same physical features, but we embrace her beauty and differences and affirm her as one of the family. This has set the tone that it is *always* safe to ask Mummy and Daddy anything.

SETTLE DOWN AND GET TO WORK

Another common issue faced by kids from hard places is a tendency toward learning difficulties. Did you know that one in four adopted children has a diagnosed disability like ADD? That's twice the rate of children raised by both biological parents (Graham, 2015).

In school, I had such a hard time sitting for long periods and was constantly in trouble for moving or talking in class. As a child—and even into high school—if a teacher came into the class and said, "OK, we have a lot to cover today, settle down and get to work," I would sit there and fight back tears. I dreaded the rebuke of my teachers and the ridicule of classmates when I couldn't sit still and be quiet in class. The genuine fear and humiliation of having. my mouth taped shut always loomed.

Let me just say that martial law never works with these kids. If a trauma child needs a break, give them one. And not on your timetable, but theirs.

ATTACHMENT ISSUES AND TRUST BONDS

Safety, security, and strong attachments are huge concerns when you are adopted. Adoptees are found to have significant attachment issues, and while I'm not surprised by the statistics, these kids are at nearly double the risk of experiencing social, emotional and developmental disorders than their bio peers, and are twelve to fourteen percent more likely to experience mental illness (Benoit, 2004).

The secure bond that normally develops between a child and her mother (or caregiver) often fails to form for adopted kids, particularly if she was neglected, abused or bounced around the foster system. It begins in utero.

So many times, people have said to me or my daughter, "You were just a baby, you don't even remember your birth mother."

Wrong. They struggle to form that kind of trusting bond with their adoptive parents and it can have a lasting, negative impact on a child's behaviour and development. Dr. Karyn Purvis wrote about the profound connection that begins between mother and child in the womb in her book, *The Connected Child*:

> *To a developing fetus, the mother's womb is an entire universe. If the mother has a healthful lifestyle, her uterus will share that with the growing child. But if the mom suffers from chronic stress, consumes toxins such as alcohol and drugs, or doesn't eat properly, the fetus is exposed to those dangers right along with the mother. An infant's neurochemistry reflects his or her very first home—the uterus.*
>
> *Research confirms that a mother's emotional circumstances during pregnancy can profoundly affect her newborn. One study found that one-month-old infants whose birth mothers were highly stressed during pregnancy had imbalanced neurochemistry. Another group of children with abnormal brain activity had birth mothers who were depressed and anxious during the last trimester of pregnancy (Purvis, 2007, p 23).*

Of course, I didn't know about the attachment theory growing up, but I experienced it. When my first son was born, as the nurse was changing his diaper, Brady cried frantically. Then, as she brought him to my arms, he quieted instantly.

I was surprised, but the nurse said, "Ah there we are! Mum's voice always soothes." She went on to explain that, from conception to birth, my voice was all Brady had heard for his entire existence.

On a subconscious level, I have always thought of it as a sense of *home*. When you are adopted, you hear a voice in the uterus, another— maybe several—in foster care, and then the forever parent.

Without continuity, where is the security? Where does the emotional bond come from? Children do not just bounce back from abuse, trauma and attachment disorder. They need serious intervention. A child's inability to form early attachments can lead them to vacillate between being too emotionally clingy one minute and then rejecting or avoiding connections the next (Benoit, 2004).

It is so important for foster and adoptive parents to be understanding and patient with their struggling child and to watch out for warning signs like anxiety, anger, mood swings, and distraught clinginess. So be warned, loving them is not enough. Because there will be days when they are very hard to love.

With Serenity, I instinctively knew that I needed to protect her, to keep her world safe and stress-free. I have had to learn to rely on those instincts and not listen to well-meaning people who offer advice that does not apply to our little girl and her situation.

One summer I enrolled her in vacation bible school. Serenity was terrified to leave me, but everyone encouraged, "Just leave her and she will be fine."

Against my better judgement, I convinced myself that she would settle down and get over her concerns. She made it through the two hours, but the price was high. Serenity was so upset with me when I picked her up that I felt terrible. Her sense of betrayal and abandonment went far beyond a mood.

Twice in the night she woke frantically screaming, "Mummy, you left me!"

I beat myself up for giving in and buckling to peer pressure like I always do. Serenity's behaviour was not bad or overindulged; it was valid and based on genuine fear. I promised her, and myself, that next time I would trust my instincts.

COPING WITH TRAUMA

If I could impress one thing upon a parent, it's this: Never back a traumatized child into a corner. I can tell you they will always come out swinging with both guns loaded. And it will always end in tears for both of you.

I was a prime example. My life was incredibly hard, like one huge battle, with everyone against me. I have carried that trauma into my adult years.

Trauma is not something you 'get over' or grow out of. Abuse, trauma and prolonged toxic childhood stress permanently changes a child's body and brain (Merck, 2018). Our bodies have a natural stress response, like an alarm, that activates a small organ at the base of our brains. It's called the hypothalamus. The alarm sets off a cascade of hormones and nerve signals; it triggers our adrenal glands to release a flood of hormones, including adrenaline and cortisol. Adrenaline is what elevates the heart rate and blood pressure with a boost of energy. Cortisol, the primary stress hormone, raises blood sugar, boosts the brain's use of glucose, and restricts unnecessary bodily functions in preparation for fight-flight-or-freeze.

What all that means is, the normal growth development and body systems—like the immune system, digestive system, and reproductive system—are all suppressed. The alarm also transmits to areas of the brain that regulates anger, fear and reason (Mayo Clinic Ed., 2019).

Understand this: children who have experienced trauma are *always in this state*. Their trigger response to fight-flight-or-freeze is always on. The long-term effects of extreme stress and excessive cortisol are harmful to the body and cause an increased risk of health problems. Just to name a few, it can cause problems with headaches, migraines, digestive issues, sleep disturbances, memory impairment, obesity, heart disease and mood disorders.

FULL CORT PRESS

During a child's peak stress response, they are experiencing *full cort*. 'Full cort' is an expression used by child development experts to refer to the full cortisol overload of the steroid hormone while they are in the fight-flight-or-freeze mode. The explosion is like a human chemistry lab. I know, because I lived it.

In fact, cortisol is necessary. It helps the body respond to an injury or illness and it balances blood pressure and blood sugar levels. But too much of a good thing is never good. So, when a trauma child's overactive adrenal glands pump too much cortisol into the body, it can stunt a child's growth, onset early puberty, trigger obesity, impair cognitive functions, and cause a boatload of other behaviour and development problems (Bergland, 2015; Folden Palmer, 2004).

TANTRUMS AND MELTDOWNS

When we first looked into adopting internationally, an agent gave us surprising advice: "Throw out whatever you learned from raising your biological children; it does not apply. These kids are different. If you use the same approach, it will not work."

Never were truer words spoken. The adoption success stories I hear of typically come from parents who understood this fact. Adoptees can be incredibly successful in their new families, but the adults in their lives must let go of the need to parent them the same as bio kids.

Who decided that this was how children should be raised, anyway? There are days that are tough, isolating and exhausting. Parenthood in general is all of this, but parenting an adopted child, particularly one with trauma or prenatal exposure to drugs and alcohol, is twice as hard. Those who take the time to really get to know their child's specific needs and challenges have won half the battle. The other half is taking action to provide supports and strategies for their child's success.

I frequently speak to despairing adoptive and foster parents who are learning the hard way not to overschedule and overstimulate their kids. Unaware that their child cannot deal well with social situations or tolerate noisy and chaotic environments in the same way as their bio peers, these parents are helpless to deal with the out-of-control reactions. These kids don't have the capacity to be thrust into every activity and event. Quite frankly, it's no good for them and—trust me—will not end well.

We need to feel safe, calm and in control. Any pressure or unpredictable situation, anything new or frightening, is like a chemical combustion that floods and freaks-out our entire endocrine system. The inevitable result is a full-on meltdown.

DISCIPLINE DOES NOT EQUAL PUNISHMENT

The typical response is to discipline the outburst of behaviour, but of course that doesn't work. Just wielding the long arm of the law sends the wrong message and will only escalate the tantrum. This child needs skills to cope, not ultimatums. Punishments will never help her navigate such volatile environments later in her life, when parents are no longer there to help her through them.

For most of my life, I hated myself for reacting the way I did in stressful situations. I felt unlovable and unworthy; that there was something wrong with me. People said I was a spoiled brat and who just needed some old-fashioned discipline. Well, I got discipline. Hell, my mum broke many wooden spoons on my butt. That kind of "discipline" was a bit like throwing gasoline on a bonfire! It never worked with me, and I don't believe that a traumatized child should have more trauma and humiliation placed upon them by punishing behaviours they have no ability to control. There is a much better way.

BE A DETECTIVE FOR YOUR CHILD

The answer is that we need to change the paradigm on handling these outbursts. My circumstances were the cautionary tale. Our family takes extreme measures, for Serenity's sake, to mitigate meltdowns in unavoidable situations. We guard her heart. We have also learned to investigate what is triggering her to avoid problems in the first place.

In order to determine underlying issues and even bring about lasting change, parents need to think like a detective; look beyond what is going on for a child in that moment. It's far more effective to diffuse a tantrum by stopping to listen, understand, and get to the bottom of a blow-up. It's essential to watch for triggers and learn the signs of a child who is about to lose it.

Perhaps adjust the circumstances by gently removing the child or help them to name and put a voice to what is upsetting them. Sometimes children cannot express themselves, or they simply don't know what is happening inside their furious little bodies. It is our job to play detective and assist them to find the words. Then we can talk to them about what we could do differently the next time.

When we started to really look past Serenity's outward actions to what she was telling us by those actions, we saw a different picture. We saw what our child was trying to communicate with her inappropriate actions. Remember, behaviour for a trauma child is always communication; it is rarely simply defiance.

THE HALT PRINCIPLE

A useful tool to help kids manage behaviour is one that has been used for many years in the psychiatric field for addictions recovery (Zomerland, 2014). The HALT principle is a self-care coping acronym using the letters HALT that is becoming a mainstream tool for parenting difficult children.

To help a child as they are becoming dysregulated, try stopping to ask these questions:

H—IS FOR HUNGRY

Is your child *hungry*? Are they reacting to low blood sugar? Children who have experienced trauma burn fat and protein three times faster than other children because of their high levels of the stress hormone, cortisol. They need to frequently eat healthy nutrients and fat-dense food.

THERAPY TIP: A great place to start is to keep snacks on hand so you're always prepared.

A—IS FOR ANGRY

Has something triggered them and made them *angry*? Often an outburst of anger usually means they are stressed, afraid or anxious because they've been put in a situation they cannot emotionally handle. This is a situation where you really need to look closely and not take their behaviour personally. *It has nothing to do with you.* They are not defying you; they are putting up walls for protection. What they have learned is anger, so they use it. Kids need a time out—not as punishment, but a chance to breathe. Sometimes the best remedy is physical activity to diffuse the aggressive energy. That doesn't just mean exercise. It means playful interaction or simple goofiness.

THERAPY TIP: If you don't have a cocoon swing in your basement, you are missing out on one of the most valuable and practical regulating tools that I have found to date.

L—IS FOR LONELY

Are they feeling *lonely*, and thus need connection? Loneliness is a clue that your child is feeling disconnected from you. Our kids want to be closer to us, even if they don't know it. Connection with our kids builds an indelible bond and reminds them that we love them when they need to know it the most. If you think they are attention-seeking, they're not. They are connection-seeking.

THERAPY Tip: Turn the TV off and put your phone down. Now is the time to stop and give them your *full* attention. Now is the time for one-on-one. Sit down and talk, read a book together, play a game. So, what, if you don't feel like it at eight thirty at night when you're tired and just want "veg out." Your child needs you to do hard things, and you may even find yourself in a better place emotionally when you go to bed.

T—IS FOR TIRED

Is your child just plain *tired?* Start with that. Trauma kids get maxed-out very easily. Social interactions are difficult for them and oftentimes simply exhaust and drain them. At this point, remove the child from the situation. If this is an ongoing issue, you should look at your schedule and edit what is not important. Do not overbook with activities or try to sneak in just one more errand. Stop immediately and give your attention to your child. It may only take that five-minute delay for all hell to break loose.

THERAPY TIP: Lots of parents say their child won't nap anymore. Don't use that as an excuse. When they are tired, they *need* rest. Try laying down with them on the bed. Bring your book with you (like this one, *just saying*) and read while they sleep. I used this strategy with Serenity, and it worked every time.

HOLIDAY MELTDOWN

Life gets busy and we want to accomplish that *one more thing* that needs to get done, so we try to stretch our child a little further before meeting basic needs. BOOM. Before we know it, we have a meltdown on our hands.

When Serenity was seven, we took a family holiday to Disneyland. In the weeks leading up to the vacation, I hadn't been feeling well. Following a traumatic car accident in 2015, I'd been diagnosed with Mixed Connective Tissue auto-immune disease (MCTD). I was experiencing a recent flare of fatigue, pain and swelling thanks to high levels of stress. Not the least of it caused by our caseworker, who had neglected to arrange for Serenity's travel documents for the trip!

Our flight was scheduled to leave in the late afternoon, so Murray said, "Let's leave at one, go through security, and then have some lunch."

I was hesitant. "I think that is pushing Serenity too hard," I said, and offered to pack a lunch to eat in the car.

Murray worried about me overdoing it in my condition, and I was secretly a little overwhelmed. I didn't really want to make lunch, so against my better judgement, I agreed.

Serenity was fairly quiet in the car. She mentioned a couple of times that she was hungry, but we assured her we would get lunch right away as soon as we got to the airport. (This was a half-lie, because first we had to drop the van at the park-and-jet, catch a shuttle to the airport, check in at departures, and navigate a long security line—all before we could have lunch.)

It was three o'clock before we made it through security and were heading toward a restaurant to finally eat. The airport was busy, and the restaurants were lined up. Awesome. After some discussion about what to do now, we sat down in the common area to wait while Murray went off to get lunch for the family.

By this point Serenity was starting to get dysregulated and totally "hangry." She became defiant and dug in her heels, refusing to sit at the same table with us. Prodding and coaxing only aggravated the situation; she proceeded to lose her nut and freaked out.

Why? Well, let's do the math: she was hungry, tired, overwhelmed, and overstimulated by far too many people and way too much noise. The situation might have been saved except for the rest of the equation: I am also a foster kid with FASD and sensory processing disorder. I was also hungry, overwhelmed and overstimulated, and here was my child defying me in public. It was a perfect storm! *Awesome.* The start of our trip was a gong show. And I was now angry at Murray—who was still innocently tracking down our lunch—because I'd decided to blame him for this shitshow.

I managed to gather my wits about me and handed Tyson five dollars to grab her some chips—yup, snack of champions. While I realized that what she needed was fat and protein, there was nothing quick and healthy on hand; I knew the snack would just tide her over until Murray returned with lunch.

Still refusing to sit with us, I had no choice but to let Serenity sit one table over and watch her like a hawk while she sullenly crunched her chips. I literally watched her hunched shoulders come down and her face soften before my eyes.

Just then Murray arrived with lunch and peace returned. In the immortal words of Seinfeld's Frank Costanza, *Serenity now!*

I don't think Murray truly understood the detrimental impact of pushing Serenity past her limits. I had always been so careful to protect her emotions and not let her become dysregulated. In his defense, Murray had never actually witnessed her melt down so completely before, because I have avidly circumvented volatile situations.

While it was a good lesson for us all, it was not the best timing. Travelling is stressful enough. Usually I carried snacks in my purse for her, but because we were crossing the border and couldn't bring fresh food, I hadn't this time. In reality I could have purchased packaged snacks, but I let my guard down and got lazy. Lesson learned.

UNDERSTANDING IS KEY

Think of it this way: if a person has an intolerance to seafood, you don't keep feeding them seafood, expecting them to get over it. No, you remove seafood from their life. Kids with prenatal exposure do not tolerate high pressure or awkward social settings the same as other kids, so *stop* putting them in those situations.

"But Sally, they have to live in the real world."

Yes, they do, but part of that is understanding what is a good fit for them, and what is not. Teaching kids how to cope will sometimes involve removing them from a situation. I have to do that for myself all the time!

My parents were loving, but they were also clueless in how to help me. Supplied with zero coping mechanisms and a brain with no filter, I stumbled through situations that I was completely incapable of handling emotionally. With no way of controlling the overwhelming rush of panic and stress that hit my body, I would self-destruct. I hated myself, but even though I wanted to stop it, I never could. Self-loathing and regret engulfed me.

As an adult, I still experience moments of sensory overload and overreact, but I know enough to try to make an exit or give my husband a cue that it's time to withdraw. I have learned, for example, that I cannot shop for long in malls. I rapidly become overwhelmed by the pushing and shoving of crowds and will literally detonate. It's not an endearing quality. Early in our marriage Murray described going to the mall with me as an "anger march."

Because of my own experiences, I can recognize when Serenity is about to shut down or "flip her lid." We do not do well when something is sprung upon us. It provokes an instant high-stress situation. Instead of making matters worse by getting angry or disciplining her, though, we do our best to understand what is overwhelming her. Whenever possible, I try to be prepared and remove her before a meltdown to save her dignity. If only my parents had known to do that for me, maybe I would not have been the hated child.

As Serenity grows older, we teach her skills to cope and incorporate strategies to help her navigate situations like these.

Here are some strategies to incorporate into your family life:

- Eating a healthy, whole foods diet with lots of *healthy* fat
- Regular physical activity, especially outdoors
- Plenty of opportunity for sleep
- Relaxation techniques: yoga, meditation, or deep breathing
- Creative exploration and crafts
- Listening to music
- Encouraging healthy boundaries
- Laughter and play

We cannot always change or avoid life's stressful circumstances, so it's essential to help our kids learn healthy ways of coping and managing the impact. This is all well and good for the average difficult child, but for the hurt brain child, we are in a whole new ballpark.

CHAPTER 8

Healing Strategies

Diet Day One: I have removed all the bad food from the house. It was delicious.
~ UNKNOWN

IF YOU THINK LOVE IS ENOUGH, I'm here to tell you it's not. There are going to be days when we are going to be very hard to love. We are desperate for someone to hear our cries. When you aren't listening, we up the ante. What I needed was acceptance, belonging and love, but I sought it in the most inappropriate ways.

That is what a child from hard places does. All we know is that an outburst got your attention. If you can look past the anger and the actions through that tough shell, beyond the tantrums and sadness, you will see a beautiful soul. You will truly see the child beneath the trauma.

History and statistics might be bleak for prenatally exposed kids to repeat the cycle set by their birth parents, but I chose to set the bar higher. I was determined to look further and fight to help my daughter achieve her best life. In my research and quest for information, I completed dozens of courses and read a mountain of books.

Just because a person has a few letters behind their name does not make them the "ultimate authority." I never allowed a so-called expert to tell me, "That's just how these kids are." They did not know *my* child. Whenever someone tells me "That's not how it's done," or "There's nothing you can do," that has *always* been my battle cry to fight. I knew that as long as I used my "FBI-level research skills" and kept looking for clues and solutions, I would find the answer to my child's needs. I would find the gold beyond the coal.

The main reason for our success with Serenity's development has been our determination to pursue answers, to continually seek new methods and treatments to help her, and our willingness to do hard things, even when it sucks. That, right there, is why we find success.

If you desire to give your child a great life, and I'm sure you do or you wouldn't be reading this, stop all the excuses. The highest word of warning I can give you is to never be in denial and simply resign yourself to the mindset that "this is how it is."

When your child is exhibiting behavioural issues or struggling in some of the ways I've talked about, it is only going to get worse as they age. If their issues are exhibiting at an early age, I guarantee that the onset of puberty will shoot it to the next level. Sticking your head in the sand and hoping that "they'll grow out of it" is a tactic destined for failure.

Denial has never worked and never will. Nothing will improve and—I promise you—it will come to bite you in the ass. You need to educate yourself on your child's trauma. These kids typically had no prenatal nutrition or supplementation, and in too many cases were subjected to a continual flow of drugs and or alcohol. We need to do everything physically possible to make up for their trauma in utero and afterward the sooner the better. Take action. They may have severe medical issues or as-yet undiagnosed complications.

What prenatal exposure did they have? What was their start in life? If someone tells you there is nothing you can do, don't believe it! There is *always* something you can do. Research the heck out of the good, the bad, and the ugly. Do everything in your power to get the support and make the lifestyle changes that will help your child. The future of your child is now down to you.

FOOD FOR BRAIN HEALTH

In my experience, most people feed their kids packaged and quick convenience meals. I get it. Family life is hectic and kids with a hurt brain are picky eaters. But there's no getting around it—processed food is crap food, none of which nourishes their bodies and especially not their brains.

As I researched the idea of 'food as medicine' to help Serenity, I was surprised by the general disbelief of even so-called experts, that diet made any difference and could have brain health benefits. The parents I spoke with claimed to try special diets that didn't help, yet when I dove a little deeper into what exactly they tried, their answers were either vague and non-committal: "Oh, I can't remember, but I know it never worked." Or harassed and defensive: "I have five kids at home so I'm too busy to fuss over food." This declaration as they sat chugging an extra-large Slurpee. Yah, I call bullshit.

REAL NUTRITION = WHOLE FOODS = HEALING

If setting up your child for failure is your goal, then I assure you, if you're feeding them the Standard American Diet (aptly shortened to SAD), you are right on track. I learned early on to not take my nutrition advice from doctors who took only thirty minutes of training in medical school.

Your child's diet needs to be clean and unprocessed to let their gut heal and absorb the nutrients in their food. Yes people, this requires old-fashioned home cooking and sticking to a more rigid plan. I know this is flipping the narrative and sometimes it's *damn hard*.

I know what it's like to still want your once a month pizza night or the Sunday drive for an ice cream cone. Cutting it out completely feels cruel, but if your child needs you to remove gluten from his diet, even so much as a piece of toast will set him back by nine months. *Nine months!* Is that toast really worth it? When we are trying to heal profound injury, there can be no cheat days.

Obviously, the younger the child when you begin making changes to his diet the better, but you can begin at any age, even with fussy eaters. That cannot be your excuse not to try. Remember, your child is not the one shopping and cooking the food. It's simple logic. If there is no junk, they can't eat it. I say this again: *this is not about you!* Either you do the hard things now, or you pay later in spades.

One of the first things that we instituted across the board for our entire family was to eat a whole foods organic diet, everything cooked from scratch. We avoid packaged food and we avoid as many chemicals and dyes as possible. We consume minimal wheat products and our bread is always home-baked sourdough.

Before eating nuts and grains, we soak them to break down the phytic acid in them, which is extremely hard for humans to digest. We supplement with probiotics, Omega 3 fish oils, Vitamin D3, and a good multi mineral. Instead of sugary beverages, we encourage Serenity to drink plenty of purified water.

As much as possible, we cook everything from scratch. Serenity loves to be involved in the cooking, and the key here is, because she helped to make it, she will eat it.

FAT FOR BRAIN HEALTH

The second they enter our world, these kids need to be supplemented with high quality fat and Omega 3 fish oils. Their brains are sixty percent fat. That means healthy dietary fats are critical for their mental health. With brains in full cort and bodies surging with the elevated stress hormones of adrenaline and cortisol (Brown, 2017), trauma kids burn fat and protein much faster than the average human. Not only that, but fats are also the vehicle that transport fat-soluble vitamins like A, D, E and K to the brain.

Our family eats plenty of good quality fats such as olive oil, avocados, beef tallow and pork lard. I recommend that if your family can eat dairy, only use *full fat* and real butter. We do nothing low fat. Serenity needs healthy fat for brain development. In fact, all kids need it, not just our kids. Contrary to the bill of goods we've been sold by the food industry and the Heart and Stroke Foundation, saturated fat is not the enemy, and there is plenty of science to back it up. FYI: The Heart Smart symbol on packaged food is not earned, it's bought and paid for.

When we began fostering Serenity at eleven months of age, we switched her over to this way of eating immediately. We focused especially on nourishing Serenity's brain with healthy fats and healing the damage done to her gut flora from the antibiotics we were mandated by children's services to use to treat her MRSA. As soon as Serenity came into our home, I started dosing her with fish oil every day. We tried a few of the quality fish oils on the market, some that even tasted great. I recommend you find one your child will take and don't ever forget to give it to them.

CHILDHOOD TRAUMA AND THE GUT

Most, if not all, trauma kids have gut issues. Up to half of adults with Irritable Bowel Syndrome (IBS) have a history of trauma or abuse (Cantor, 2019). A recent study of young foster and adopted kids linked the separation from biological caregivers and other childhood trauma with certain brain functions that relate to mental and emotional health, as well as disruptions of their gut microbiome. The study specifically referred to gastrointestinal issues of constipation, stomach aches, nausea, and vomiting in children under preschool age (Cantor & Technology Networks Editors, 2019).

Serenity had the worst case of constipation I have ever seen. She would not have a bowel movement sometimes for two weeks, and then it was painful and rock hard. The pediatrician prescribed RestoraLAX, an over the counter (OTC) laxative, for six months. Feeling pressured by the fact that we were still fostering and had no say in her medical care, I reluctantly agreed to put her on it. After a week, Serenity's behaviour changed drastically.

When I started researching into it, I learned that Polyethylene Glycol, the active ingredient in RestoraLAX, MyraLAX, and several other OTC laxatives, is a neurotoxin that has been reported to cause "neuropsychiatric events" and behaviour changes, and in some cases even Autism (Monastyrsky, 2012).

Autism?! Are you kidding me? Not even RestoraLAX recommends the medication for children or pregnant women, and certainly not for more than a week, even for adults.

Fortunately, there was no permanent damage as a result of the *malpractice* of Serenity's pediatrician. Within two days of pulling her off the medication, she was back to our darling girl. Never again! I knew then that we were on our own.

A conversation with another parent, whose child also suffered from severe constipation, mentioned having success with using digestive enzymes. We began using the natural supplement daily before meals. Guess what? An eleven-dollar bottle from the health food store addressed a serious problem we had been dealing with for three years.

As a next step, we searched for recommendations for a functional practitioner who would consider the whole child, not just symptoms. The naturopath we located began working with Serenity to detox her liver, and her general health began to improve wonders.

Unfortunately, the very moment she was diagnosed with Epilepsy and was placed on seizure medication, Serenity's health plummeted downhill almost immediately. All our progress with the naturopath was eliminated and we were back to square one.

HEALING BEGINS IN THE GUT

Have you ever heard of the term "leaky gut?" The medical condition is referred to as intestinal permeability. That is what happens when our food is not properly broken down in the stomach, tearing microscopic holes in the intestine walls and allowing putrefied stuff to travel right to the bloodstream. Not a pleasant thought.

This toxic exposure and gut inflammation can lead to dysbiosis, which has been long recognized by the medical community to cause digestive diseases like IBS, celiac disease and Crohn's disease (Campos, 2017/2019).

There are many daily contributing factors that can cause a disrupted microbiome, from the use of antibiotics, to the consumption of foods sprayed with insecticides. Even unfiltered tap water can be detrimental to our microbiome. Studies are now showing that it is a contributor to all manner of autoimmune diseases, from lupus, arthritis, and multiple sclerosis, to asthma, allergies and obesity (Campos, 2017/2019).

Surprisingly, it is even a contributing factor to mental illness. Scientists are examining the connection between the gut and the brain (called the gut-brain-axis) and are finding a link with the emotional and cognitive centers of the brain. This indicates that disruptions of the gut microbiome can lead to depression and anxiety disorders, schizophrenia and even autism (Clapp et al, 2017).

It's pretty clear, even if it's not easy, the first thing we need to do is heal the gut. In as little as twenty-four hours, studies have shown that making simple dietary adjustments can impressively alter the balance of gut bacteria (Clapp et al, 2017).

GETTING STARTED IS THE FIRST STEP

Along with cleaning up the family diet, this means incorporating plenty of probiotic (fermented) and prebiotic (fibrous) foods that will repopulate good bacteria in the gut. With every meal, include fermented foods like kimchi, raw sauerkraut, or kefir. I recommend avoiding most grains, which are hard to digest, and have been sprayed with insecticides. Also, steer clear of most dairy, which is loaded with antibiotics. And an incredibly gut-healing food that is also delicious to drink every day, is bone broth. I found it was super easy to make, and for many years I have been cooking our own.

One of the resources that we used with Serenity was *The Gut and Psychology Syndrome,* by Dr. Campbell-McBride. The author lays out her 'GAPS' diet to fix an impressive list of conditions, including ADD, autism, dyslexia, dyspraxia, schizophrenia and depression. Now, full disclosure, the program was fairly intensive, but at the time, we found that it really helped to begin healing Serenity's leaky gut.

FOOD OBSESSIONS AND ADDICTIVE BEHAVIOUR

Learning that I was denied the basic necessities of life as a newborn, that I'd come with broken bonds to my new parents as a starved and neglected baby, affected me significantly and shaped how I began to view everything in my life. The psychological trauma has manifested in different ways along my journey.

I was an infant though … how could I possibly remember being starved?

Regardless of whether an experience is in your recalled memory, it remains locked in the subconscious during the childhood developmental years. The repressed memory is part of the survival mechanism (Seltzer, 2019). To a child who has been starved, food is everything. It is survival. It is life. And it represents love.

Not surprisingly, I developed some addictive behaviours associated with food. Surrounded by a thin and athletic adopted family, I was neither. Comments about my weight and the amount of food I ate plagued me constantly. These were never helpful and spoke more harm than good. Unrecognized as a core trauma, my food obsessions and weight were continual issues growing up.

"Are you sure you should have that?"

"Do you really need that much?"

No, apparently, I was just a pig.

If you notice an obsession in your child, the worst thing you can do is make a production out of it. For their sake, get to the bottom of it, instead. By changing the foods they eat, and beginning to heal their gut, you will organically address the weight issue.

Most certainly, I would advise against ever commenting on their weight or limiting their access to food. Putting a child with food issues on a 'diet' will only make matters worse.

Trust me, I know. I lived it. I thought about food all the time, and as an adult I recognize a tendency toward food hoarding in times of anxiety and stress. I cannot remember a time when my love-hate relationship with food was not front and center in my world. The lack of food as an infant meant I was not loved, so naturally, food was how I received love. Later, cooking became how I showed love.

I would hate going out for supper because I was scared there wouldn't be enough. In my university days, when friends were gathered and we'd decide to order pizza, we would all pitch in a few bucks. I can remember the minute I handed over my money, I would begin to stress about not getting enough.

I fought an inner battle to keep that fear monster at bay, and truthfully, I still do, although I recognize it and can laugh at my food hoarding habits. There have been many jokes in our home regarding some of my grocery shopping quirks.

Murray has said to our boys, "If Mum goes to buy corn, for the love of God, stop her. We have enough in the freezer to stock Costco!"

Once it was limes. Once it was bread. Then there was the sweet potato affair of 2015. I go through weird obsessions and fixate about not having enough. The item will vary from month to month, but it is always there. At any given time, I have a stockpile, and the fridge needs to be full at all times or I feel anxiety and palpable discomfort when it is not. In self-reflection, it seems ridiculous as I write the words, but that does not change the reality or the need of my compulsion. Food is security. Food is love.

Food becomes a really huge issue, especially for a child who has been deprived. They will always be worried about not having enough to survive, and will manifest in hoarding behaviours, even if there is enough. Their hunger is at the core of their subconscious. Many adoptees and foster children grow up to be overweight or obese because food becomes so pivotal to their psyche. These are deep wounds that need to be addressed early, if possible.

One strategy for people with food deprivation issues is to have something non-perishable in their room to have as "insurance." There is safety in knowing the food is always available, and that they will never have to go without again. Most likely, they won't even touch it. It's not about hunger, it's about felt safety. For that reason, I always leave a bowl of fruit on the table that is free for the taking. The kids may or may not eat it, but it is there as insurance.

COUNSELLING AND THERAPY

There are some effective therapy options available, but you have to seek it out. As I have said, for adults, I am not a huge proponent of 'talk therapy.' When you are dealing with trauma, I have found that simply talking about the past only tears open the wound and drags up the pain, without really addressing it or rooting it out. Talk only devolves into wallowing in self-pity and it leaves you there.

For me, it led to deeper anxiety and depression rather than bringing any kind of healing. I've mentioned my psychologist, Kim, who is a rare gem among therapists. Instead, her clinical approach has been an integration of specialized therapies that truly work.

I believe a better option for children might be to find a therapist who practices play therapy. This is a tactile and integrated program designed to develop strong attachment bonds between a child and parent or caregiver. It is accomplished through specific games and creative play together with a child.

I would caution you from putting all your eggs in one basket, though. Many modalities are needed to heal our kids. Not all modalities work for everyone, so this will be a bit of trial and error.

SUPPORT GROUPS (AKA BITCH SESSIONS)

I have met many couples who were at their wits end, not knowing where to turn next. Some of these encounters were in support groups for foster and adoptive parents. Sometimes I felt I was going through this alone. Surely there were other people who were going through the same struggles as me.

I began to search out support groups, hoping to collaborate with other parents who had maybe gone before me. I found one group, but I would not have called it a *support*. The parents were there to complain and one-up each other on which of them had the worst kid.

The reality is that we need to fight for our kids. It's not easy, and honestly, most kids are hard work. When you get those little successes, it is such an amazing feeling that it makes up for the moments when you just aren't sure how much more you can take. Be very careful of the support groups that devolve into bitch sessions. They almost always come down to comparisons of who's got it worse. This negativity is never in the best interest of either you or your child, and it will never be part of your child's healing story.

Moving from coping to thriving requires us to *stop* doing a few things. For starters, stop bitching about your kids. Stop focusing on what's wrong and work toward becoming a problem solver. This means finding support that is centered around solutions. Negativity only breeds more negativity and bears no fruit. I promise you; a positive focus will always improve the situation and yourself.

Secondly, stop comparing your child to other children, and stop looking at milestones that your child may or may not be achieving in comparison to their peers. All kids are different. Comparing is a dangerous game that only leaves a person feeling depressed and defeated every time. Instead, focus on what your child has achieved. What does your child do that cracks you up? What things do you most love about your child?   Rejoice in them. Remind yourself of these regularly.

Children who need the most love and understanding often ask for it in the most unlovable ways. Always look for the sweetness and the humour, because some days it is hard to find.

BUILDING CONNECTION

You need to know this: *your child can be bonded to you, but not connected to you.* I have seen this over and over again. Your kids are connection-seeking, but they don't know how to get it from you. They will be bonded to you because they live with you and you are familiar. Yet, while they may love you, they may not be connected to you.

Connection is the holy grail of parenting. If your child is truly connected, you become their go-to and their soft place to fall. Children from care have had to parent themselves and often their siblings. They need to believe you will meet all their physical and emotional needs. When there is connection, their anxiety and fear diminish.

The key is true connection. But you cannot simply schedule quality time. It must be *intentional*, but it has to happen organically. To give you an example, one night, after an exceedingly long and stressful day with my son, Tyson was supposed to be getting ready for bed. I tried to hurry him along, and he made one of his typically funny and sarcastic comments.

I warned, "Tyson, not tonight!"

He was standing inside the pantry. Without a word, Tyson suddenly grabbed three mini marshmallows and threw them at me.

They hit me smack on the nose. Something in me snapped and I dove for the marshmallows.

What ensued was an epic twenty-minute marshmallow battle with both of us hysterically laughing. All crappy moods were over; all air of a fight was gone. Both of our stomachs hurt from laughing so hard. This was real, unscheduled connection with my seventeen-year-old son. The kitchen looked like a blizzard had struck, and it took until midnight to clean it up, but neither of us cared. To this day we still talk about that night.

We have a saying now, when things could potentially escalate: "Do you need me to get the marshmallows?" and it makes us laugh, diffusing whatever the conflict.

YOU CAN'T OUTSOURCE CONNECTION

Something important we have to remember about connection with our kids is that we have to do the work. We cannot simply hire someone else to do the connection piece. We have to do it ourselves. It's long and arduous. There are days when we might feel like we're taking one step forward and two steps back, but we keep on going; before we know it, we've mastered the foxtrot.

I met a young man named Bryan (not his real name) whose daytime gig was being a companion to two boys with severe neurological disabilities. Bryan was hired to make those connections with the boys, so their parents didn't have to. Granted, his involvement was a great addition to their quality of life, overall, but it did nothing for the relationship between the boys and their parents. All it did was let the parents feel 'off the hook' for the hard stuff.

The parents missed the point entirely. There should never be a Bryan in your child's world until they are truly connected with you.

That should never be part of your connection strategy. Your kids don't need Disneyland; they need you.

NEUROLOGICAL REHABILITATION

You'd be surprised how often I have heard people say that the disorders our kids are dealing with can't be fixed. "It's permanent brain damage," they told me. "Their brains are full of holes like swiss cheese."

I could have shriveled up in despair, and accepted that fate for myself and my daughter, but if you've read this far, you already know that's just not how I roll. If you say it can't be done, I say, "Watch me!" Enter brain balance treatment (which is the bomb—by the way).

You've probably heard the old adage that people who are right-brained are creative while left-brained people are more logical and analytical. For years, parents and teachers have encouraged activities that strengthen one side or the other of the brain, but psychologists and scientists are starting to learn that when one side of a child's brain dominates over the other, the result is dysfunction in various forms.

I first learned about brain balance through an incredible book by a Neuropsychologist named Dr. Robert Melillo. Intrigued and excited, I searched out a local practitioner of the program. When Serenity was three years old, we located a centre in our own area and took her through the neurorehabilitation treatment program with Dr. Will Farrell.

Neurological rehabilitation is all about retraining the left and right hemispheres of the brain to communicate. Dr. Melillo, who is an expert in childhood neurobehavioral disorders, is the author and architect of the Brain Balance Program. He coined the phrase 'functional deficiencies' to refer to the myriad of disorders from ADD to autism and everything in between. Both hemispheres must work together, so a balanced brain is essential for effective motor skills, information processing, and a healthy digestive and immune system (Education.com editors, 2013).

Children who have a left-brain delay struggle with writing and language processing. A right-brain delay can look like clumsiness, poor motor skills and poor posture. Dr. Melillo's book, *Disconnected Kids*, provides incredibly detailed tests and exercises that parents can perform with their child to determine what delays they may have (Melillo, 2009). His twelve-week program is outlined in the book to allow families to try it at home, but it is franchised all over the world by licensed practitioners.

For Serenity, the neurorehabilitation treatment program was life changing. We watched our three-year-old develop before our eyes. Prior to the program, she used to switch hands with her chalk while writing on her chalkboard. I was surprised to learn in the brain balance material that this was not normal, healthy development.

Within a few weeks of treatment to build neural pathways in her brain, both hemispheres began to "talk" to each other and she no longer did this. The biggest change we noticed initially, was that Serenity stopped responding frantically to the doorbell ringing. This alone was a game-changer. Neurorehabilitation takes intense commitment and specific daily exercises, but we found it is worth every effort.

As Serenity has grown older and begun to display different learning challenges with her schoolwork, we found it beneficial to revisit those neurorehabilitation exercises to stimulate communication between both hemispheres of her brain. This periodic treatment may be continual throughout her life; we learn and discover the process as we go along.

GRIEVE THE LOSS

One of the hardest things for us parents to grasp is that no matter the circumstances, we all must learn to grieve the loss of what we thought it would be. We all have preconceived notions of what we thought parenthood would be like, and let me tell you, as a parent of three kids, I have had to do this at every step of the way. So many of the visions I had about my family looked nothing like reality.

As a control freak who wanted everything perfect, this was super frustrating for me to grasp. Even a simple family photo shoot would turn into a gong show when, no sooner had I dressed up my kids in their Sunday best, that someone would fall and rip their clothes or be smeared with a giant dirt stain across one cheek.

And then there were the bigger issues.

Both of our sons struggled with learning differences. When Tyson was younger, we discovered he had ADD. For Brady, unfortunately it wasn't until high school that he was finally diagnosed with dyslexia and dysgraphia. After struggling through all his school years as though (in his own words) reading Chinese, he was tested just in time to be able to have the exam support he needed to succeed in his final exams.

Having laboured through their early school years to read, write, and study, neither boy had any desire to go to university. I dreamt of Brady becoming a big-time entrepreneur, but that was so not his thing. At this point, I have to let that dream go.

Our children will most likely not turn out how we imagined, and that is okay. We have to stop taking our children's behaviour and actions personally. It is not an affront to us as parents. It's not even *about* us. So much of the conflict that takes place between us and our kids is because we have placed huge—and often unreasonable—expectations upon them. They, quite literally, cannot conform to what we want them to be.

People are scared of going against the tide. Changing course from what they've always done, or what everyone tells them to do, isn't popular. It doesn't win friends. But does that matter? We aren't here to make our friends happy; we are here to do what is best for our kids.

One of the worst statements I always hear is "Well, that's the way we've always done it."

If what we are doing is not working, then STOP.

We need to look harder, deeper, farther. We need to keep trying new techniques and new strategies, because the mainstream just does not work with our kids. Making the choice to foster and adopt were not popular actions, either. *Too bad.* What matters is doing the hard things that will allow our children to thrive and have an amazing life.

And what that amazing life looks like for each child will look different in every family. For one parent, it might be that their son becomes a lawyer, for the next it could be that their son is clean and sober. We need to stop using other people's kids as a measuring stick for our own. Comparison is the thief of joy. By grieving the loss of what we thought it would be, it allows the freedom to be open to what is possible. *Let. It. Go!*

CHAPTER 9

Legacy of a Broken System

The difference between stupidity and genius is that genius has its limits.
~ ALBERT EINSTEIN

* * *

A WISE PERSON ONCE SAID TO ME: "If you do not lead with love, then everything else is lost." Children are not disposable. No matter what the circumstance, we are not a lost cause. As I get older, my youthful arrogance fades and I recognize that the more I know, the *less* I know. I constantly seek out and learn new information in all areas of my life, which is why I have zero-tolerance for people who think they already have all the answers. From my perspective, those people are the most ignorant because they have stopped learning.

When you combine *chosen* ignorance with the scale of power wielded by an institution like social services, all at once you have a very dangerous brew. The system may be necessary, but it is arguably flawed and broken. From the highest levels of soulless government decision-makers, its misuse of power and bureaucratic red tape leave a legacy of human debris in its immovable, ideological wake. Was that damnation too harsh? I don't think so.

WHAT'S WRONG WITH THE SYSTEM?

There are so many childless couples who would be desperate to raise these kids, but by the time they are eligible to be adopted, they are so incredibly damaged by social services that most people are put off. Then, if someone does still manage to follow through, they are so ill prepared for what they're about to encounter, that they often throw in the towel, anyway.

The reality is, potential foster parents are grilled like criminals, and have many of their rights stripped away by a complete invasion of their lives. There is literally no question social services will not ask. One of our prequalification questions asked Murray and I about the quality of our sex life. *What the heck does that have to do with anything?* My response was "none of their damn business."

Until you navigate the foster system, you probably have no idea how horrible and broken it is. Those that remain as foster workers for long periods of time don't seem to question the long-term ramifications of what this system is doing to these children. They have not researched what trauma does to a child. They do not recognize how subjecting babies and small children to mandatory bio parent visits continually break a child's connection bonds and is actually quite disturbing for the child.

You do not have to go far in a Google search or on social media to discover the incredibly detrimental long-term impact of childhood trauma, yet social services cannot acknowledge the major role they play in perpetuating the wounds that a child in foster care endures. They have the remarkable ability to take an already atrocious situation and make it horrifying. Why does the child have absolutely no rights? Why does child welfare keep going backwards in their practices? I say, if you are not willing to be part of the solution, then move over and get out of the way.

FOSTER, NOT CARE

Foster care *does* make a difference for the children and families that it *helps*, but make no mistake, the impact on the child is a double-edged sword. Foster care is *not* a home. It would never be a child's choice. In most cases, foster care is a temporary stopgap that simply transfers a child from unsafe biological parents into dispassionate childcare, and then right back 'home' again. I would argue that bouncing kids through multiple foster homes is *never* okay.

In fact, social services makes no effort to be nurturing. The mandate of the foster system is merely to provide children with the essential food, shelter, clothing and education. But meeting basic needs is only half of the picture. It meanwhile neglects the child's emotional well-being and need for bonding.

As evidence of this, one of the barbaric practices within social services is to temporarily hold an apprehended child in a hotel room while social workers shift in and out. Already a victim of traumatic circumstances, these terrified children are further violated, with no emotional stability, or any possible way to form safe, healthy bonds with a caregiver. This is not *care*. It is an extension of the abuse.

COPING IS NOT RESILIENCE

I despised it when social workers said to me, *"Kids are resilient."* That's a cop-out statement meant to whitewash the harm and neglect they perpetuate on the kids in their system.

Yes, children who have experienced trauma may appear to be incredibly resilient, otherwise we would not be survivors of our own holocaust. But make no mistake about it, coping is not resilience. Coping is certainly not thriving. Most people equate resilience to rolling with the punches or rebounding from a set-back. The dictionary says, it is the "ability to recover from or adjust easily to misfortune or change" (Merriam-Webster, 2020). With all due respect, the mistreatment and wounds our kids have endured are far more than punches and setbacks, and they most definitely do not "adjust easily to change."

Kids who are forced to go on visits with drug addicted bio parents they barely know, do not forget. Kids who have been raped, beaten and starved, do not adjust. Is *resilience* really the word that applies here? This is severe trauma, and they do not just get over it. Trauma does not just disappear when a child is removed from an unsafe home. It lurks in the background waiting to rear its ugly head. Denial does not make it go away. Trauma forever changes who these kids are and is extremely difficult to heal from. They learn to cope, and some of their coping mechanisms are brilliant, but most often they are destructive. The trauma must be addressed in ways that help children move beyond merely coping to truly thriving, and that takes work.

YOU WON'T LEAVE ME THERE?

When our family was moving to our current house, Suzanne—Serenity's foster nana—offered to take her overnight so we wouldn't have to keep track of a little one underfoot. Since we'd begun fostering, Serenity had never slept anywhere except at home, so I thought we had better have a practice run. She was excited when we talked it over, and when the day came, Serenity eagerly packed her bag. As we drove, however, she got very quiet. I glanced in the rear-view mirror to check on her.

"Are you ok?" I asked.

"Mummy," She said quietly, "You will come back for me, right? You won't leave me there, will you?"

I nearly pulled the car over. After all this time, enveloped in our love and security, this little girl was still scared and insecure. She still wasn't totally certain of her place in our family. It broke my heart. I reassured her that she was my girl and, of course, I would be blazing a trail back to her! I told her how much I loved her. I have to reassure her all the time. Explain to me how "resilient" she is?

Those same social workers could technically have said that I was resilient, but I know a truer story. Being fostered and adopted myself, I learned firsthand what kind of devastation results from trauma. Born on the fetal alcohol spectrum, I was neglected, abused, judged, bullied, and raped. I've got more letters than doctors with PhDs: PTSD,

FASD, ADD, MCTD ... Like every other trauma kid, I learned to be on my guard against unsafe people.

ON HIGH ALERT

When you're a trauma kid, you are always on high alert. I am frequently accused of being too emotional or sensitive and that I wear my heart on my sleeve. The implication, I assume, is a weakness. Instead, I consider that one of my greatest strengths.

True, I take things personally and tend to have a trigger response in stress, but I know this: *I am anything but weak!* And neither are our kids. People *do* hurt us, and people in authority do not always have our best interests in mind. So, of course, I am always watching for it, and that is why I have become a badass warrior for Serenity and other kids like her.

As wards of foster care, we have *never* had a voice. We don't need Band-Aids and platitudes. We want to be heard! That means we need a revolution. Those in charge, making decisions under the guise of "what is best for us," need to be called out. Law makers, judges, social workers, bio parents, and so-called experts all must be held accountable for the damage they are doing to children on a daily basis. No, they are not saving kids; they are damaging the next generation and perpetuating the cycle of abuse that they have been tasked to correct. It's important to know the beast before you can tame it, so let's talk about what's wrong with the system.

UNDERMINING FOSTER PARENTS

As in any organization, there are all kinds of foster parents, each with their own motivations. Foster families endure an onslaught of intrusive scrutiny and challenges to their parenting practices, no matter how constructive or innovative. Often, they are treated as mindless, paid mules who are questioned for any deviation from the government script. This both undermines their honest desire to serve and perpetuates the ugly stereotype of Agatha Hanigan's greedy head mistress of *Little Orphan Annie* fame.

OK, the comparison is extreme, but I have personally witnessed what amounts to a baby mill, where foster parents use the system as a means of profit and are in it solely for the money. Fortunately, that is not the case in most foster situations. Unfortunately, often those who truly have a heart for fostering, and are instinctively good at it, end up burned by the system and drop out. Worse, if they—like me—stray from the strict script by attempting to improve the lives and healthy development of a foster child, it does not go unpunished.

Granted, some foster homes are placed with a child that is simply too much to handle, often with special needs or a complicated medical diagnosis. The problem lies in a lack of proper training for these foster parents.

LACK OF SUPPORT

Typically, foster parents are ill prepared to take on a foster child. Many of whom have already suffered more trauma in their little world than most people ever endure. Any support and instruction from child welfare is minimal and does nothing to equip families.

When we began our journey from foster-to-adoption, we had big hopes and dreams. Naturally, we wanted Serenity to have a great life and to raise her to become the best she could be. Our efforts were thwarted every step of the way by domineering caseworkers and discouraged by disinterested support workers. Their basic training course was outdated and utterly useless; there were no resources from current experts, and it did not include new research. Instead, the material was saturated with hopeless and defeating phrases like, "these children will only be able to..." and "this is the way these kids are." Their so-called 'tools' provided absolutely nothing practical to improve Serenity's welfare. The only useful information or tangible help came through my own determined research.

SET UP TO FAIL

Why do so many foster care placements fail? Why do kids who spend their childhood with a stable, healthy family still—*inexplicably*—end up repeating the destructive cycle of their biological parents? Because trauma, neglect and abuse are cellular. You cannot just feed, clothe and shelter a child and think that will be enough. You cannot discipline or structure out ADD and FASD. I repeat: *what works with bio kids does not apply here.*

The major reason for failure by far is Child and Family Services itself, with its policies and programs that play such a detrimental role. At a time when the security and development of foster children is so critical, they desperately need *all* the cards in their favour. The sad part of it all is that in one hundred years of providing social services, the child welfare system has not improved. Child services still hands over severely injured foster children to unequipped families. Though they are quick to share a laundry list of dysfunctions and medical conditions for these kids, they offer zero hope to change their futures. When a placement fails, it is yet another loss for a child. For heaven's sake, we want more for these kids than to merely keep them out of jail or prevent them from getting pregnant.

What foster families need is to be equipped with a completely different kind of training. Here's a wild concept: What if parents were empowered to counteract the effects of trauma? What if their parenting was encouraged to be trust and connection-based and not consequence-based? What if, instead of medicating young children into oblivion, we could employ *real* experts with treatments that actually work? What if, instead of complacency and pseudo support programs like respite care, we give families tangible resources and *hope*?

RESPITE CARE

Of all the programs intended to support foster parents, one of child welfare's big go-tos is respite care. Regardless of the philosophy of respite, it is not actually for the child. To be patently clear here, this program is for the caregivers.

It would be short-sighted not to recognize that sometimes having trained care workers available to a foster parent is essential. Even bio parents hire a babysitter or leave their kids overnight with grandparents or friends. In an emergency or difficult situation, where could a foster family turn without this resource?

Our family has never used respite care. Fortunately, we maintained our relationship with Serenity's foster nana and papa who cared for her from infancy. I will concede that ability to have childcare for a few hours has been invaluable, especially when Serenity was terrified to stay with anyone else. But respite is a *temporary* intervention. To expect it to be the sole solution is foolish. Problems don't magically disappear when everyone returns home. Most certainly, not for the disrupted child, who already has issues with attachment and insecurity.

Real trouble with respite care arises when it is misused and overused. Repeatedly pulling children from the safety they know, to linger a week or more with a complete stranger, does not put her needs first. Neither do foster parents who frequently use these programs for their own interests. That's when respite care starts to toe a fine line between support for caregivers and neglect of foster children. And it raises a huge red flag.

THE BATTLE FOR RIGHTS

The fact is, foster and adopted children have zero rights and little say in all this. Listen, I understand to a degree how we got in this mess. Over fifty years ago when I was apprehended, within a month I was placed for adoption. I was the fifth of six children born to this woman, but even so, that was abrupt action.

Child welfare has been criticized over the years for violating parents' rights. Now, at the expense of a child's rights, the pendulum has swung to the other side. In my opinion, they have veered so far from their original mandate to help children, that they have lost the plot along the way. Who is defending the rights of the child? Did their protectors forget—or perhaps turn a blind eye—to the fact that their arbitrary policies are damaging children as deeply as negligent or abusive parents?

When I needed my adoption history, it was kept under lock and key by my government. I could not understand why I was not afforded the same rights as every other Canadian. How was it that the prior right of my birth mother came before me, an adopted child? It was truly barbaric that I had no control over my own life and information.

In many states and provinces there are adoption registries where a biological parent may consent to submit family medical histories that can be made available to adopted children, but there are still hoops to jump through, especially when the identity of the parent is kept from the child. Go back to that last sentence...did you catch that important phrase? *A biological parent may consent...* Even when a system is put into place for the sake of the child, it's not their right that takes precedence. The primary right is still that of the bio parent. What about the child's rights? Why do we have to justify why we need this information? Why do we need to prove to some pencil-pushing bureaucrat that we have a right to know who we are and where we came from?

BIOLOGY IS NOT ALWAYS BEST

I am actually grateful that my birth mother did not keep me. In spite of the abuse I experienced and the sense of not belonging, I fully recognize that my life would have not been better had I remained in my birth home. I have met my birth mother and trust me, I was grateful that she didn't raise me.

Child welfare's mandate is to return a child to bio parents, or at least extended family, whenever possible. I get that efforts to maintain a family unit are well-meaning, but there are just some situations where living with biological parents would actually be more damaging.

Remember, the child in question was removed for a critical reason. They pay an awful price by being transferred back and forth, while repeatedly giving ineffectual chances to their bio parents. Sure, there are rare cases where this actually works, and I am happy for those mothers and fathers. In far too many situations though, the loss of their child must, unfortunately, become yet another consequence of their actions. If the needs of the child are not the primary consideration, everyone loses. I reiterate: *biology is not always best.*

LET'S TALK ABOUT BIRTH MOTHERS

Within the foster care system, birth mums are wounded, naive, and typically in denial. Those who believe they will get their child back, rarely succeed without major efforts and changes on their part. Though their hearts may be in the right place, they are often clueless to what they're doing wrong.

In Serenity's case, her birth mother thought that all she needed to do was get off drugs, but that was only half of the problem. At only a few days old, Serenity was apprehended from a crack den. Her mother, whose previous children were also in foster care, had no basic life skills and suffered from FASD herself. She would also need a complete overhaul of friends and family influences.

Social services and other agencies could provide all the tangible support to empower her to actually thrive, but she would literally have had to remove all unhealthy influences from her life, which in her case would have meant her entire family. The systemic, familial and cultural problem went back generations. The odds were so incredibly stacked against her.

When Serenity was four years old, her bio mother gave birth to yet another child who, like her previous siblings, was also immediately apprehended. Even though child services clearly recognize she is incapable of parenting her children, they continue to bounce them from family to foster care, and repeatedly put them through the terrible ordeal of mandatory visits.

I do not think birth mothers should be floating in and out like the wind, just in case one day she can take them back. This may seem cruel to the bio mother, but trust me when I say this, these scenarios are *never* in her child's best interest.

MANDATORY BIO VISITS REALLY MESS UP KIDS

What people need to understand is that the mandatory visits are never actually for the child. They are *always* about the birth parents, and their rights supersede all else, most often to the detriment of the child.

Children are in the foster system for a lot of reasons. Their parents either did not or could not do the job of raising them. I can tell you, as a foster child, and as a foster parent myself, there is no benefit and very little bond for the child. Visits with a bio parent they don't even know is like meeting the strange lady across the road. It means nothing to them and is actually quite distressing.

In the first years of fostering Serenity, I sat through so many mandatory visits with her as she fought against being placed into the arms of her birth mother. She cried and clung to me for dear life. Her birth mother was so hurt; she was a stranger to her baby.

This concept is one of the hardest for a birth mother to understand and to not take personally. Her own flesh and blood does not know her and is *afraid* of her. It is a heartbreaking thing to process; very often she cannot deal with it.

When Serenity was still a preschooler, we had to disconnect our doorbell. Every time it rang, she would panic and run screaming for Mummy. Nothing could settle her until I picked up her trembling little body. She clung so tightly that I could barely breathe. Why? Because she was convinced it was a driver from child services coming to take her away for a mandatory visit.

This is what the foster system did to Serenity. Strangers arrived at our door to drive her alone to visits with parents she didn't even know. The stranger hysteria continued for years, long after Serenity's adoption was final, and there were no more required visits. The uncertainty of unfamiliar situations made her feel unsafe and anxious. She couldn't relax and enjoy any outing or social engagement because she always worried whether I was nearby. I lost count of the times I sat on a cold gymnasium floor while she had yoga or a homeschool gym class. So many of the swimming lessons I paid for were a bust, because every few seconds, she was looking back to make sure I hadn't left her.

Serenity's situation wasn't nearly as grim as what so many kids have to endure, but to say I have strong opinions on mandatory bio visits would be an understatement. For once in Serenity's whole adoption process, I think it should have been about the child, and only what's best for her.

REUNIFICATION WITH BIRTH FAMILIES

For whose benefit is the Temporary Guardian Order or the Permanent Guardian Order with visitations continued? What is the rationale for continuing these dreadful and disruptive visits if the biological parent will never get the child back?

Why do we continue to torture both of them? When a viable adoption is preferable for the child's sake, why is this not the goal? Shouldn't we be moving heaven and earth to *truly* save these kids?

The reason is that the system is set up to always favour birth parents. Child welfare's mandate of reunification is a doctrine that supersedes the rights and best interest of the child.

When a birth Mum has gotten pregnant with her sixth child, is still using drugs, and hasn't managed to break free from her unsafe lifestyle to get back any of her kids, why then does the system keep giving her repeated opportunities at the expense of her children? I agree that she deserves rights and respect, but at what point do her second, third, fourth...twentieth chances supersede those of her innocent children? The rationale is that she must be given the opportunity to change.

Again, I agree; everyone deserves an opportunity to learn and grow and change. In fact, practical training and tangible supports should be available to her. But I must ask the hard questions... when do her children stop being the victims of her choices? When do children like Serenity get a chance? When are they allowed to feel safe, to breathe easy, to feel loved? When do they get their chance to bond with a forever family? These powerless kids should not be forced to deal with adult problems and forever pay for the mistakes of their parents.

LET'S TALK ABOUT SOCIAL WORKERS

You don't have to go far to hear horror stories of the foster system. Decisions are made daily within child services by people who are either unqualified to make them or are so bound by bureaucracy that their loyalties are misguided. Dreadful experiences for foster parents, and appalling accounts of kids being sent back home to abusive parents are unfortunately commonplace.

We are talking about small human beings who, through no fault of their own, are placed in horrific situations. They pay an unspeakable price when screwed-up adults fight over who has the rights to them, and when child welfare repeatedly fails to give their needs precedence. When a social worker admits that it is "never about the kids," you have to wonder. *Well then, who is it about?*

Social workers are just messed-up, flawed human beings like the rest of us mortals, but a huge part of the problem is they don't realize it. I have categorized them into three types:

THE POWER-TRIPPER — These tyrants bulldoze through your home like they own it, sweeping the proverbial white glove for figurative dirt. They have seen it all, and their currency is intimidation. Every day they deal with negligent parents and delinquent kids. You're all the same, just here to milk the system. Well, not on their watch! They just *know* you are hiding big secrets and they can't wait to pounce. They believe in the rightness of their actions, because their trust is in the iron-clad justice of their encyclopedia of policies and procedures. *Rules at all cost,* *and children be damned.* Coldly official, every encounter with them is a horrible experience. Bullies, when confronted, either attack or back down. The best way to handle the power-tripper is to stay strong and stand your ground. Despite their distrust, you know who you are. They are hired civil servants, after all. Our first social worker was a power-tripper of the first order, confronting me on everything. Harassed and afraid, I meekly took her browbeating until she crossed a line and something inside me snapped. When I let her know she wouldn't be allowed to intimidate me and refused to take her crap, I was respectful, but firmly within my rights.

THE PAYCHECK COLLECTOR — These complacent civil drudges have done it all, seen it all, blah, blah, blah. They were idealists once. They wore their heart on their sleeves and it was broken too many times. They cared once upon a time, but the stress and defeat and endless cycle of futility has built up a wall of apathy. Now, they are blind to the stress and struggle of hardworking foster parents. They are immune to the tears and fears of the kids under their careless watch. They plod and shuffle, accomplishing the bare minimum to punch the proverbial time card and check out. Here is the one golden rule for working with the *Eeyore* of social workers: learn when to kiss ass and when to kick ass. When you wake them from complacent slumber, they remember why they signed up for this impossible gig, and for a brief window, they will be your ally.

THE DEDICATED SOLDIER — Those who truly care about the kids are the rarest of breeds; they have a beating heart! Dedicated and compassionate, they have not forgotten why they came to social work in the first place. They desire to make a difference for hurting children and they want to help you succeed. Even when their agency too often ties their hands, and they feel defeated by the endless futility, they soldier tirelessly on. I met only a few throughout the entire fostering and adoption process of our daughter, but I truly appreciate them. They will do whatever is in their power to help you, but just as true soldiers, they always obey their commander. Don't take advantage of them—they aren't pushovers. Trust and respect goes both ways. The fact that dedicated soldiers exist is the reason for a sliver of hope that there can be change in child welfare.

THE LAND OF FEAR AND INTIMIDATION

When we began our fostering journey, I was so desperate not to risk losing Serenity that I tried pathetically to please every social worker. The helpful caution to not "piss off" my worker, left me fearful of making mistakes and risking their ire. Well, I am here to tell you, that no matter what you do, in the eyes of the power-tripper, it will always be wrong, and she will delight in pointing it out.

I was quite literally terrorized by fear and intimidation. Repeatedly, they used an abuse of power to control and manipulate us. Not for Serenity, but for themselves and their own egos.

Within the system, experiences of being threatened and bullied is so common that one might wonder if the tactic wasn't written into some barbaric training manual. *No one* has a right to do this. The second I became angry, I took my power back, and everything changed. Murray and I requested a new support worker and eventually asked to be moved to another governing office.

Sure, I was labelled as "difficult." I probably even (gasp!) pissed them off, but I'm ok with that. Because they are critically wrong about something. It really *is* about the kids. It's about Serenity.

A LETTER TO SOCIAL SERVICES (AKA MY CATHARTIC RANT)

DEAR CHILD AND FAMILY SERVICES,

You wonder why I take issue with the child welfare system and its autocratic drones? Why, you ask me? Here is where the disconnect happens for me: I hate people who hurt kids.

I'm not going to sugarcoat it anymore. Child abuse is despicable and evil. I lived it. It deserves the word *hate*. While we sit here and quibble over harsh words, children are being systematically abused. Every day, caseworkers see the atrocities happening to kids, yet they make inexplicable judgement calls that contribute to the ongoing exploitation. These children and youth are not disposable. They are human beings.

Let me remind you of a few of the actual decisions you've made on behalf of them:

- Ripping a boy from a wonderful home with loving foster parents, who were in the process of adopting, only to place him back with his bio mother who demonstrated her 'love' by duct tapping his sisters to a chair for her boyfriend to rape. But it's okay now because "she doesn't have that boyfriend anymore."
- "Reunifying" a child, for the third time, to a mother who sits back and does nothing while her child is beaten and abused.
- Apprehending kids to safety from an alcoholic and passed-out mother on the report of a neighbour, only to return them after mum's 19-day rehab. (That same 'fit' mother who, on the same day she got her kids back, called a babysitter so she could go out partying.)
- Being fully aware that a struggling single mum with a newborn

is using her three-year-old to help parent the baby and doing nothing to stop it.

- Mandating four different antipsychotic drugs for a four-year-old boy when dietary changes could have made a huge difference instead.

- Authorizing a male social worker to take a child into a bedroom—*alone*—with the door shut and refusing the parent to be present. That, my dear social services, is called 'grooming.'

Children in foster care are the most vulnerable victims in our society; they are the most sex trafficked children on the planet. There are ten million children in the sex trafficking industry and most of them are in the foster care system. Why? Because nobody cares about them. Nobody is watching. Nobody is paying attention.

This, dear social services, is just a sample of the so-called 'good' that your child welfare system is doing. Shame on you! The question that you should be asking, dear social services is, "Would these be the right decisions for my own children and grandchildren?" No?

When you go home at the end of the day, dear caseworker, do you turn a blind eye and pretend the atrocities are not happening? How do you sleep at night? How do you block the images of finding an infant in a drug den, starving, cold, and covered in her own filth?

Is it just another day at the office? Is it just a job? A paycheck? How do you flip that switch in your brain?

Is it a graduation requirement of your oppressive, apathetic, and handcuffed child welfare workers to perform a surgical procedure to remove the hearts? Is that why decency and ability to exhibit human kindness is so noticeably absent? Where did all that go? Because, trust me, you are not doing the good in the world that you set out to do.

Your actions—*and lack of action*— make you just as guilty as schoolyard bullies, perpetuating the abuse. At best, you run around ineffectually putting out fires. What we need is for you to *prevent* the fires. You have a long way to go to *truly* help the thousands of children in your foster system.

Dear social workers, check your egos at the door. Get your head out of your ideological clouds and start making decisions that *actually are* in the best interest of the children you claim to protect. Stop enmeshing your decent caseworkers in government bureaucracy and arbitrary policies. Untie their hands and allow them to truly make a difference. Re-educate every employee and root out the toxic weeds. If you cannot change it from the inside, then maybe it's time to get out.

Something has to give. If you, dear social services, are not part of the solution, then you are clearly part of this *enormous* problem. Every day, you perpetuate this global pandemic of abuse. For the sake of our vulnerable kids, and their desperate families, enough is enough! Wake up, it is time for change!

CHAPTER 10

Changing the Narrative

I used to think I was the strangest person in the world, but then I thought there are so many people in the world, there must be someone just like me who feels bizarre and flawed in the same ways I do. [...] Well, I hope that if you are out there and read this, know that, yes, it's true I'm here, and I'm just as strange as you.

~ FRIDA KAHLO

✳ ✳ ✳

INSTEAD OF HOPELESSLY RESIGNING OURSELVES to accept that kids from hard places will never amount to anything, or that the best we can do is hope they stay out of jail, it's time to change the conversation and look for solutions. I have found, and worked with, many experts in their various fields who are changing kids like Serenity for the better.

Did you see what I said there? *I have found... They exist!*

Why in the hell was I not told about them by child services when we began fostering? Why are they not employing these experts who are discovering (and proving) there is hope for our kids? *A lot of hope.* There is so much recent research in early intervention for kids with ADD, FASD, dyslexia and autism spectrum, just to name a few.

CHANGING THE MINDSET ON HOPE AND HEALING

As I mentioned in Chapter 8, therapy programs, like that of the Brain Balance Centers, are producing amazing results by retraining the left and right hemispheres of a child's brains to 'communicate' and develop new neural pathways where they were damaged. Even changes to dietary protocols have begun to show dramatic improvement for diagnosed children.

These are *real* strategies to address, and even counteract, what your child may have endured in the womb and beyond. Our family has witnessed firsthand the good they can do by how much they are changing the outcome for Serenity.

CHANGING THE MINDSET ON FOSTERING

There is something (ok, many things) that has bothered me from the outset of our fostering journey. What's with the pervading belief that kids from foster care have less value or that they are somehow disposable?

Shortly after we started fostering Serenity, Murray lost his job, and we found ourselves with a few unexpected and expensive house repairs. I shared with a friend that we were struggling financially and emotionally.

She said, "Well, maybe now is not the time to take on another child!"

Really? That's an acceptable answer to our difficult circumstances? Discard an inconvenient child?

"If I was pregnant," I asked her, "would you have told me to have an abortion? Why didn't you get rid of your child when your husband recently lost his job?"

Her startled response told me volumes. "But he is my son!"

Maybe she thought we would just give her back. My brain could not compute that Serenity was somehow disposable. *Replaceable.* I took offence on every level.

What kind of despicable human being could bring a child into their home to care for, only to casually send them back? *No.* If anything, Serenity (and every foster child) is deserving of *extra* love and compassion.

CHANGING THE MINDSET ON ADOPTION

Except in rare circumstances, adoption is seldom the first action that people take when deciding to raise children. As a couple, Murray and I chose adoption. The perception that we have settled for second best is reprehensible, and yet, that has sometimes been the implication. Equally obnoxious is the suggestion that we are somehow heroes and saints for having 'rescued' Serenity's life. The presumption is that she should be fawning in gratitude to us for the home and family we have given her and therefore act accordingly.

All of these mindsets, in my opinion, are not just false; they are ludicrous, and need to change.

Adoption is both wonderful and complicated. Yes, there are challenges, and a lot of information and preparation is essential. But regardless of whether or not an adoptive parent is able to have a child biologically, adoption gives them and the child an incredible opportunity. Not because anyone is a hero, or should be grateful, but because together they are a family.

If you had told us that we would be adopting from child services, we would have said you were crazy. Adopting from the foster system did not seem like a viable option. Let's be honest, we'd heard the horror stories. We worried about dealing with the health consequences of a child with trauma, FASD, and who knew what else.

Over fifty years ago, when I was in foster care and placed for adoption, people were unaware of how much damage alcohol and drug abuse had on an unborn child. If they suspected any issues, social workers would make up a sweet story, so the child wasn't considered "unadoptable."

In complete contrast, foster and adoptive parents are now bombarded with so many potential problems and worst-case scenarios, that many just get skittish and walk away.

Another important consideration for families is choosing interracial adoption, though it has become much more common. It's an added factor with its own set of obstacles but doesn't have to be a barrier. Adoptive parents, who are intentional about teaching their interracial child about her culture and ethnicity, are better able to help her establish a healthy identity. Actually, I would argue that it is more important to create a diverse environment that is accepting of *all* races and cultures.

Fostering to adopt has been, for us, one of the most amazing gifts and life-altering lessons that our family has ever been through. When I first sensed God nudging us toward adoption, I felt it rather fitting. I was coming full circle. Who better to understand and connect with an adoptee than me, another adoptee?

After our disappointing attempts at adopting privately and internationally, our little girl literally fell onto our laps. I knew it was divine intervention. The minute my husband and I met Serenity we knew her adoption was meant to be. We knew she was ours.

CHANGING THE MINDSET ON BIOLOGY

There is so much emphasis on preserving the biological family of foster children. The mandate of Child and Family Services to reunify a family unit is idealistic at best, but to maintain that it is *always* the best situation for a child is ludicrous. If only that were true, we wouldn't need the foster system.

Capacity to breed does not even remotely qualify a person to raise a human. Parenting means sacrificing for your children. Our children need love, but love is not just an emotion. It is also an *action*. Love means putting your own needs second. It means rocking a child for hours through a bout of colic. It means holding them when they are sick and wiping up puke at three in the morning. It means staying home from fun social events. It means sleep deprivation and all-night vigils in a hospital room. Love means doing the hard things.

Reunifying a child with a parent who will not—or cannot—do this, is not only cruel and irresponsible, it is another form of child abuse. All this back-and-forth business damages kids for life and reduces their chances of getting a forever home, because the more wounded they become, the harder they are to care for. This is why we have an epidemic of damaged and traumatized children in foster care. Biology is such a small piece of the family picture. What matters is commitment, self-sacrifice, and love in action.

CHANGING THE CYCLE

Sadly, most foster kids in care go on to repeat the same disastrous cycle as their bio parents, especially those who 'age out.' The statistics are daunting to the point of almost losing hope. It stops here. I am determined to break the cycle for Serenity. If I can make a difference in just one life, then I have succeeded. By sharing our story—and motivating others, I hope—I am working toward change.

At what point do we all say enough is enough? If we are not helping, we are increasing the damage. It is time to start putting the needs of the kids first. The message that child welfare needs to hear is this:

- Stop moving children from foster home to foster home. It is disastrous and damaging. It prevents their ability to truly bond to anyone.
- Stop sending children back to unsafe environments and abusive caregivers.
- Prepare families for the role they are taking on and provide them with genuine support.

CHANGING THE MINDSET OF BROKENNESS

I've heard some people refer to their adopted kids as being born 'broken,' as if they think this will somehow be inspiring for other parents. In fact, there is a book by that title, written by adoptive parents, about their internationally adopted son. *Born broken?* Is that really the legacy they want for him? That they thought of their child as broken?

Broken says there is something essentially flawed and unacceptable. Broken says less than. How demeaning and demoralizing for that boy, and quite frankly, any child. I resent the implication that I, also an adoptee with challenges, might be considered broken and in need of fixing to be acceptable.

Both of our sons struggled in school with learning challenges, Tyson with ADD and Brady with dyslexia and dysgraphia. When Tyson would get frustrated at his inability to focus, I would always tell him that ADD was his superpower. He was easily distracted because his lightning fast brain left the rest of us swirling in his dust. Instead of giving up and accepting his so-called limitations, at age twelve, he was building websites for international clients. By seventeen, he was working in the film industry. Now, at only nineteen, this clever young man thrives in an amazing job as a cinematographer within the marketing and media industry. We didn't make his ADD a problem, we made it a potential!

After our oldest was finally diagnosed in high school, I asked Brady how he felt about it. His response nearly broke my heart.

"Well on the one hand I'm sad," he said. "Because now I am labelled. But on the other hand, I am glad there is something actually wrong, and I am not just stupid."

My response was immediate. "Let me be clear, my boy. There is nothing wrong with you. Your brain just processes things differently, and that is completely ok."

It was never a measure of his competency or worth as a person. Brady was—and is—brilliant. He simply learned in an extraordinary way. The boy who needed a reader and scribe to pass high school, ended up acing his college degree and now, with his lightning sharp memory, has a successful career in IT.

The same applies to all of us children from hard places. *We are not broken*. We process things in an extraordinary way. The key is to stop putting the stigma of 'damaged goods' upon us, and for heaven's sake, stop saying we are broken!

LOOKING FOR ADVICE IN ALL THE WRONG PLACES

Everybody has an opinion on fostering, adoption and raising kids. Even me! And everybody, especially family, seems to feel the need to express those opinions each time you turn around. What Cousin Sven or Aunt Matilda or your brother Edwin did with their biological child is frankly irrelevant and most likely wrong for your child. Their "constructive" criticism only makes you feel like a failure. When you get caught up in a negative headspace it can be really easy to feel like you're getting nowhere and that not even your family understands.

But the worst thing that foster and adoptive parents can do is arrogantly assume they have it all figured out. *You do not have this! How could you?* Foster kids and adoptees need ten times what you think you know, and ten times more than your undying love. The people that struggle with their child typically have not made those distinctions. And then, when they're in deep waters, these same parents grab any and all life rafts. The one life raft that I guarantee is full of holes is child welfare. They prove time and again that they have zero clue about how to break the cycle of foster care, or how to truly help kids caught in their system.

A word of caution about all the free advice. Do not take it from someone who has not been in your situation. To paraphrase Dr. Brené Brown from her well-known *99U* talk: *If you're not in the arena getting bloodied, sweaty and dirty, I'm not interested in your opinion* (Brown, 2013).

Here's the advice you need to hear: Your kid is not a hopeless case. They can be functioning members of society. They just need the tools, support, and unconditional love. It is up to you to look for solutions. To become your child's detective and become the authority for your child's specific needs. The issues are often obvious when you truly pay attention.

CHANGING THE WAY WE PARENT

Isn't it time we changed how these kids are cared for and parented? If we were doing it right, parenting kids from hard places would look like nothing anyone has ever seen.

Over the years, people have commented on how Murray and I are raising Serenity. They have admonished us on what we're doing wrong with her medical care, her food, her schooling, and most often, her closely guarded social activities. I always ask them to remind me again how many traumatized foster kids they have raised. *Oh, that's right...none.* I no longer try to spare their feelings. Until they know what they are talking about, they can put a pin in their opinions.

Our kids need us to advocate for them. They need someone who has their back one hundred percent of the time. They need someone who is prepared to piss a few people off to protect their hearts.

Lead with love people! When you lead with unconditional love, your child will know that you are always there for them. *That* is the message they need. That they are loved, no matter what. And that they will always have a soft place to fall.

CHAPTER 11

Serenity Saved Me

The way I see it, if you want the rainbow, you gotta put up with the rain.
~ DOLLY PARTON

✳✳✳

THIS JOURNEY THROUGH FOSTERING AND ADOPTING our daughter has unexpectedly taught me so much about myself. Not just about how I came to be, but *why* I am the way I am.

I'm glad I was adopted. Being adopted was not a curse. I understand the magnitude of what I escaped by being apprehended, as did my daughter. I am still that little baby whose biological mother drank during her pregnancy. I am the child who was apprehended into the foster system because that same mother starved and neglected her. I am still the little adoptee who endured unspeakable sexual abuse. I know all this, and I recognize the impact it all had on my psyche. But now I am on the other side. After spending my whole life being what everyone wanted me to be, I have finally gotten to the place where I don't care anymore.

Along the way, I learned why, even on my best days, I was the unruly child that no one particularly cared for. I finally *get* why I come out swinging when I'm backed into a corner. I can forgive myself for not being able to cope calmly and rationally to situations in the same way as others. I can forgive myself for my terrible potty mouth; it is kind of like turrets. I just say the wrong shit all the time and I can't stop myself. At fifty-five years of age, I can finally cut myself some slack. Most importantly, I can stop hating and beating myself up for what I had no control over. I can finally breathe.

There is something hardwired in my brain that is determined to fight back if you tell me I can't do something. It's like double daring me! *Game on—just watch me do it.* This was both a blessing and a curse for my whole life. The consequences that ensued, in order to prove people wrong, usually led to self-destruction. I played hard, partied hard, and burned the candle at both ends. But there have been times in my life when my determination has helped me accomplish things that everybody said I couldn't.

The screaming in my soul pushes me on, even though people often think I'm crazy. Being pig headed did not win me friends in the foster system, but I realized early on that I was not in this to win a popularity contest. It was for one reason only. Serenity. The stakes were high, but this time the fight was to make sure Serenity felt safe, loved and to be able to live her best life. I made it my life's goal to stop allowing fear to let me play small. Obstacles be damned. People defy the odds all the time, why couldn't we?

Truth be told, Serenity has saved me. I see so much of myself in her that some days it scares me. We experience the same thoughts, feelings, and insecurities. I see her painful shyness one moment and then her cheeky attitude the next. I sense her underlying apprehension of not being safe and the fear that we will abandon her. It haunts me, because I still live with those anxieties.

Who am I?

Where did I really come from?

Why am I here?

Where do I fit in?

Why was I not enough?

All the unanswered questions linger like haunting lines of music stuck in my head. I know Serenity feels all these things, too. I see it in her eyes, and often in her words, but mostly in her actions. She clings to me, but I love the opportunity to hug her and be her comfort. I love this child with a force I cannot explain. She is my girl and I am her Mum; biology cannot change that. Please know that I would die for my boys, but with Serenity it is different. She needs me in a way they never have. Because I have been there, I *get* her. And, because of Serenity, I am starting to *get* myself.

We are an odd pair, Serenity and I, yet we are one in the same. We have a whole host of secondary issues, but together we also have a level of connection like no other. I understood, when we adopted Serenity, that we could not treat her the same as our bio sons. She needed a different approach. She needed *more,* and that is a fact.

One of the biggest mistakes I saw adoptive and foster parents make was to think they knew what the hell they were doing. I'm an adoptee, and yet I knew enough to know that *I didn't know enough.* I had to get educated on how to help my girl. Why? Because after struggling all my life, I knew I did not want that for Serenity.

I made it my mission to guard her heart. So much of my intuition comes from having lived what Serenity is living. No one understands an adoptee better than another adoptee. I wanted to do for her what was *not* done for me. Maybe because my birth mother neglected me, and my cries were ignored, I've spent the rest of my life screaming to be heard. Now that I have found my voice, hopefully you will hear it and understand. I want Serenity to be heard and understood, too.

I see so much of myself in Serenity. I *understand* why she flips out over loud noises and abrupt changes to plans. I *know* why she craves assurance of her identity. I *feel* intimately the need for safety and security. As she grows to become a young woman, I want to be her safe haven, a place of love, acceptance and understanding. I want to be her soft place to fall.

It is because of this child that I can look back and discover all this about myself. This child, who came to us by some crazy miracle, has changed my life in ways that I never thought possible. She is the other piece to my puzzle. *Why am I here?* Because Serenity needed me. *Why is she here?* Because I needed her. The puzzle pieces fit.

I am Serenity, and she is me. Two lost souls who needed each other. Through her eyes, I found a reason to love myself and seek a greater understanding of who I am. Because of her, I finally found myself. It has taken all these years of searching, and adopting a child just like me, to finally realize it. Serenity has saved me.

RESOURCES

Recommended Programs

Family Hope Center: familyhopecenter.com
FASD Workshop with Jeff Noble: fasdforever.com
Empowered to Connect Parent Training: empoweredtoconnect.org
Brain Balance Achievement Centers: brainbalancecentres.com
Neurorehabilitation Treatment: drwillfarrell.com/treatment

Recommended Reading

The Whole-Brain Child, by Dr. Daniel Siegel and Dr. Tina Payne Bryson
Disconnected Kids, by Dr. Robert Melillo (Creator of the Brain Balance Program)
The Connected Child, by Dr. Karyn Purvis
The Primal Wound: Understanding the Adopted Child, by Nancy Newton Verrier
The Gut and Psychology Syndrome, (GAPS Diet) by Dr. Natasha Campbell McBride
The Out of Sync Child: Recognizing and Coping with Sensory Processing Disorder, by Carol Stock Kranowitz
Parenting from the Inside Out, by Dr, Dan Siegel and Mary Hatzell
Attaching in Adoption, by Deborah Gray

REFERENCES

✳ ✳ ✳

CHAPTER 4

Gonzales Gompf, Sandra. (n.d.). MRSA Infection Symptoms, Treatment. Infectious Disease Health Center; MedicineNet.com. https://www.medicinenet.com/mrsa_infection/article.htm

CHAPTER 6

CDC. (2020, May 7). CDC: National Center on Birth Defects and Developmental Disabilities. "Fetal Alcohol Spectrum Disorders: Basics about FASDs." Centers for Disease Control and Prevention, Atlanta. https://www.cdc.gov/ncbddd/fasd/facts.html

Klintsova, A.Y.; Scamra, C.; Hoffman, M.; et al. (2002). Therapeutic effects of complex motor training on motor performance deficits induced by neonatal binge-like alcohol exposure in rats: II. A quantitative stereological study of synaptic plasticity in female rat cerebellum. Brain Research 937:83–93. National Institute of Health, Bethesda. https://pubs.niaaa.nih.gov/publications/aa63/aa63.htm

Olson, Heather Carmichael and Montague, Rachel A. (2011). Prenatal Alcohol Use and FASD: Diagnosis, Assessment and New Directions in Research and Multimodal Treatment; "An Innovative look at early intervention for children affected by prenatal alcohol exposure." 64-107. Department of Psychiatry and Behavioral Sciences, University of Washington School of Medicine, Seattle Children's Hospital Child Psychiatry Outpatient Clinic, Fetal Alcohol Syndrome Diagnostic and Prevention Network, Families Moving Forward Research Program, and Seattle Pacific University, Department of Clinical Psychology, Seattle. https://depts.washington.edu/fmffasd/sites/default/files/

CHAPTER 7

Graham, Ruth. (2015). Why Adopted Children Still Struggle Over Time. The Atlantic, Boston, MA. https://www.theatlantic.com/health/archive/2015/12/adoption-happily-ever-after-myth/418230/.

Benoit, Diane, MD FRCPC. (2004). Infant-parent attachment: Definition, types, antecedents, measurement and outcome. Paediatric Child Health. Oxford University Press. National Library of Medicine: National Institutes of Health. Bethesda, MD. https://www.ncbi.nlm.nih.gov/pmc/ articles/PMC2724160/

Purvis, Karyn. The Connected Child: Bring hope and healing to your adoptive family. McGraw Hill: New York (2007).

Merck, Amanda. (2018, February 6). "4 Ways Childhood Trauma Changes a Child's Brain and Body." Salud America. https://salud-america.org/4-ways-childhood-trauma-changes-childs-brain-body/

Mayo Clinic Editorial Staff. (2019, March 19). "Chronic stress puts your health at risk." Mayo Clinic. https://www.mayoclinic.org/healthy-lifestyle/stress-management/in-depth/stress/art-20046037

Bergland, Christopher. (2015). "How do various cortisol levels impact cognitive functioning." Psychology Today. Sussex Publishers. https://www.psychology today.com/ca/blog/the-athletes-way/201506/how-do-various-cortisol-levels-impact-cognitive-functioning

Folden Palmer, Linda. (2004). Baby Matters: What Your Doctor May Not Tell You About Caring for Your Baby. Sourcebooks, Naperville. [excerpt found at: https://www.naturalchild.org/articles/guest/linda_folden_palmer

Zomerland, Godrun. (2014, June 7). "H.A.L.T. (Hungry, angry, lonely and tired): a self-care tool." HealthyPsych, LLC. https://healthypsych.com/h-a-l-t-hungry-angry-lonely-and-tired-a-self-care-tool/

Conger, Krista. (2007, March 7). Stanford Report: "Sever Stress hurts children's brains, changes hippocampus, study shows." Stanford News; Stanford University, Stanford. https://news.stanford.edu/news/2007/march7/med-carrion-030707

Guarino, GinaMarie. (2017, May 30). Mental Health and Attachment Issues. Wickenburg, AZ. www.claudiablackcenter.com/adopted-children-often-face-mental-health-struggles-as-young-adults/

CHAPTER 8

Brown, Arianne. (2017, December 3). "What is adrenaline and how does it work in our bodies?" Biostrap, Los Angeles. https://biostrap.com/blog/what-is-adrenaline-and-how-does-it-work-in-our-bodies/

Cantor, Carla. (2019, April 1) "Gastrointestinal complaints in children could signal future mental health problems." Columbia University, New York. https://news.columbia.edu/news/gastrointestinal-complaints-children-could-signal-future-mental-health-problems

Cantor, C, and Technology Networks Editors. (2019, April) Childhood trauma can impact our gut bacteria." Technology Networks Limited, Sudbury, UK. https://www.technologynetworks.com/neuroscience/news/childhood-trauma-can-impact-our-gut-bacteria

Monastyrsky, Konstantin. (2012, December). "Is MiraLAX the next Vioxx? The role of MiraLAX laxative in autism, dementia and Alzheimer's." Gut Sense, Lyndhurst. https://www.gutsense.org/gutsense/the-role-of-miralax-laxative-in-autism-dementia-alzheimer

Campos, Marcelo. (2017, September 22; updated 2019, October 22). Harvard Health Publication, "Leaky gut: what is it and what does it mean for you?" Harvard University Medical School, Cambridge. https://www.health.harvard.edu/blog/leaky-gut-what-is-it-and-what-does-it-mean-for-you.

Clapp, M., Aurora, N., Herrera, L., Bhatia, M., Wilen, E., Wakefield, S., Clin Pract. (2017, Sept 15). "Gut microbiota's effect on mental health: The gut-brain axis," 7(4): 987. doi: 10.4081/cp.2017.987. US National Library of Medicine; National Institute of Health, Bethesda. https://www.ncbi.nlm.nih.gov/pmc/articles/PMC5641835/

Seltzer, Leon F. (2019, December 4). Psychology Today, "Subconscious vs. unconscious: How to tell the difference." Sussex Publishers LLC, Sussex and New York. https://www.psychologytoday.com/ca/blog/evolution-the-self/201912/subconscious-vs-unconscious-how-tell-the-difference

Education.com Editors. (2013, May 1). "Brain Balance: Tips for a 'full-brain' workout." Education.com, Inc., a division of IXL Learning. https://www.education.com/magazine/article/brain-balance/

Melillo, Robert. (2009). Disconnected Kids: The Groundbreaking Brain Balance Program for Children with Autism, ADHD, Dyslexia, and Other Neurological Disorders. Perigee Books, New York.

CHAPTER 9

Meriam-Webster.com (n.d.). "Definition of resilience: 2: an ability to recover from or adjust easily to misfortune or change." Meriam-Webster, Incorporated. https://www.merriam-webster.com/dictionary/resilience

CHAPTER 10

Brown, Brené. (Dec.4, 2013). 99U: Why your critics aren't the ones who count. 99U Conference. https://brenebrown.com/videos/99u-why-your-critics-arent-the-ones-who-count/

About the Author

✳ ✳ ✳

SALLY J KING is an author, speaker, advocate and family coach. As an adult adoptee from the foster system, Sally knows firsthand the devastation of childhood trauma. She is a survivor in more ways than any one person should ever have to count, but has learned that the only way out is to go *through*. Her passion to give a voice to the vulnerable and voiceless has caused her to advocate for change in the foster system, and has become a message of "Healing, Help, and Hope" to families who are struggling. A parent of three, two bio sons and a daughter that she and her husband adopted through the foster system, Sally embraces her duty to "do the hard things" to ensure her children grow up with a secure foundation and a strong sense of self.

Connect with Sally J King:

Website: sallyjking.com
Instagram: @sallyjking
Facebook: facebook.com/sallyjking

Please take time to write a book review!

If you enjoyed this book, let me know! Take a few minutes to write a review on the platform where you purchased it. Your review really helps others to find this book. Thank you!

Books by Sally J King

In Search of Serenity: *From Foster Child to Adoptive Mum*

LunchBox Love

Printed in Great Britain
by Amazon